Advance Praise

You, Me, and Anxiety takes the reader on Dr. Robyn Reu Graham's personal journey as she shares her guidance, knowledge, faith, and action plan on how to live with and manage anxiety. There is no holding back Robyn's truth, love of her family, and her faith. She reflects on her struggles with anxiety with an unwavering desire to enhance the lives of young women so they can be mentally and emotionally healthy throughout their lives. She is an absolute inspiration to everyone that has ever felt even the slightest tinge of anxiety, self-doubt, and wonder.

DAMIANN BILOTTA, FOREVER FROSTY FOUNDATION

What a powerful read! As a psychotherapist, I'm excited to have *You, Me, and Anxiety* in my toolbox to help my clients and their teenage daughters. On a more personal level, I'm blown away by the beautiful vulnerability that Robyn brought to this book. Her courage in sharing her story will absolutely empower others to experience their own journey through anxiety differently.

ELLEN FELDMAN, PSYCHOTHERAPIST AND AUTHOR OF *A PATH OF ONENESS*

After all these years of waiting for the "parenting an anxious child while you're an anxious parent" handbook to arrive at my doorstep, I can finally stop waiting! This handbook has arrived, and it's been created in such a comprehensive way. Dr. Robyn Reu Graham shares with us a teen and parents edition plus a workbook/journal to support readers to "do the work" even when they aren't feeling particularly motivated. Robyn's writing style is relatable and authentic. As a parent of two anxious teens, I felt like she was talking to me as I read through the pages of the parents' edition. This body of work is going to change lives for generations to come. This book will make a huge difference for anxious teens and their parents!

EMILY GOLDEN, MCC EXECUTIVE AND
CAREER COACH, AUTHOR, SPEAKER

Growing up struggling with anxiety came with a lot of challenges. *You, Me, and Anxiety* contains a collection of things I wish I was told earlier, and, as a reader, gives me the validation and comfort that we often do not receive from others.

KAYLA MERCHIORE

Robyn provides excellent advice on how to manage anxiety and live a full life from the perspective of a person that has lived with anxiety her whole life.

CONNIE JO MILLER, MOM OF A DAUGHTER
WITH LIFE-LONG ANXIETY

As a college student who suffers from generalized anxiety disorder that has only been exacerbated by the pandemic, *You, Me, and Anxiety* allows me to feel heard. While managing your anxiety is certainly easier said than done, this book provides you with feasible options to do so. I am so impressed by how much useful advice this book has given me that I can apply to my everyday life.

JULIA PEREZ, BSN CANDIDATE IN NURSING WITH A MINOR IN NUTRITION, UNIVERSITY OF PENNSYLVANIA

There are a lot of people who live with anxiety throughout their lives, they just learned how to manage it. This book reminds the reader that there is no shame or judgment for having anxiety, whether you have anxiety or a loved one has anxiety. Managing anxiety is not an easy task but with practicing CBT, one can program their brain to manage their anxious thoughts. I really like Robyn's 5Cs journaling method and it's a great tool to have for when uncertainties or stress arise. This book educates, empowers and brings hope to people and their loved ones who are struggling with anxiety. I also like reading Robyn's personal stories and how her experiences made her who she is now—a kind, empathetic and driven woman.

MARIA REYES, M.S., PROFESSIONAL TRAUMA COUNSELOR

You, Me, and Anxiety is an excellent book for teens and parents to help navigate the struggles of anxiety and everything that it involves. Dr. Graham shares her own journey with anxiety in such a real and relatable way that as a teacher and certified school counselor, I highly recommend this gem of a book.

MELISSA ROCKOVICH, M.ED.

In *You, Me, and Anxiety*, Dr. Robyn Reu Graham endeavors to connect with her readers (and her former teenage self) with a uniquely personal narrative. The book is a raw, authentic, and hopeful portrayal of her life living with anxiety. While not a mental health professional, Dr. Robyn Reu Graham weaves practical recommendations for coping with anxiety into her personal narrative in a very down to earth and readable format.

RUTH ROSENBERG, M.D., PSYCHIATRIST

After all these years of waiting for the "parenting an anxious child while you're an anxious parent" handbook to arrive at my doorstep, I can finally stop waiting! This handbook has arrived, and it's been created in such a comprehensive way. Dr. Robyn Graham shares with us a teen and parents edition plus a workbook/journal to support readers to "do the work" even when they aren't feeling particularly motivated. Robyn's writing style is relatable and authentic. As a parent of two anxious teens, I felt like she was talking to me as I read through the pages of the parents' edition. Robyn, this body of work is going to change lives for generations to come. Thank you for sharing your gifts so generously. You are making a huge difference for anxious teens and their parents!

This book is meant for every age and every stage of life. Anxiety manifests itself in many forms, in many ways and in many people. I only wish I had this incredible resource in my teen years, in college, in law school, after giving birth for the first time, while parenting teens, and at many other stages of my journey. This book is simply a must-read teaching how one can take ownership of their own life and be the hero of their own journey, just like Dr. Robyn.

GINA F. RUBEL, ESQ, CEO, FURIA RUBEL COMMUNICATIONS, INC. AND ONRECORDPR.COM PODCAST HOST

In this engaging and helpful book, Dr. Robyn Reu Graham explores the roots of anxiety and provides practical strategies on how to create lasting change. Not only will readers find actionable tools and resources, they will also receive encouragement and understanding. Dr. Graham's personal struggle with anxiety gives her a visceral understanding of what it's like to grapple with anxiety, and her resilience and ultimate victory provides hope for change. The information and inspiration in these pages are sure to help anyone who wants a roadmap to leave anxiety behind and live a life of confidence and freedom.

DR. NINA SAVELLE-ROCKLIN, PSY.D.

Anxiety is a problem for people of all ages. *You, Me, and Anxiety* offers readers practical ideas and actual steps to better manage this potentially disabling emotional experience. Robyn's openness about her journey is inspiring. This book stands on its own and can also be a valuable addition to any professional treatment plan.

JENNIE SCHOTTMILLER, LICENSED MARRIAGE AND FAMILY THERAPIST

After thirty years of helping individuals and parents manage anxiety in themselves and their children, I have read a lot of books on this topic. Dr. Graham's *You, Me and Anxiety* is going to be one I recommend to my clients moving forward. She writes with such warmth and empathy. The book offers an understanding of what anxiety is, how it presents, what it truly feels like, as well as specific ways to manage it. The author includes real life stories and examples as well as techniques and scripture. The result is a valuable resource for any parents or teens struggling with anxiety. This book could not have come at a better time!

> KIM SWALES, PH.D., PARENTING COACH
> AND PODCAST HOST OF CONNECTING
> WITH DR. KIM SWALES

Great piece to help assist you in combatting anxiety. This book offers great insight and tips to help slow down your thinking and evaluate the root of your anxiety.

> SAM TRAFFORD, COLLEGE STUDENT

Dr. Robyn Reu Graham is the hero in her own journey, understanding and managing anxiety. She teaches us the 5Cs journaling method, which is a wonderful step-by-step process to come through anxiety, better and stronger than before. I will use this book as a reference for the thousands of teens we counsel each year, during some of the most difficult periods of their young adult lives.

> MICHELLE VEIX MCCARTAN, FOUNDER,
> FORWARD COLLEGE COUNSELING

As someone who struggles with anxiety every day, this book helps the reader to feel less alone. This book gives different perspectives and opens the eyes to what it's like to live with anxiety. As well as this book dives into techniques and ways to cope with anxiety. If you are struggling and feel lost or want to educate yourself on anxiety this is a great read for you.

NATALIE R. WAUGH

I thought I knew about anxiety, but I was very wrong. After just reading the first three pages, I knew I had to dive headfirst into re-learning. If you have someone you love or even yourself that suffers from anxiety, this is a must read. Robyn makes it feel like she is talking to you, comfortable, warm, honest and helpful.

TRISHA WAUGH, PARENT AND ANXIETY
SUFFERER

You, Me, and Anxiety

You, Me, and Anxiety

TAKE ACTION OVER ANXIETY TO ENJOY BEING YOU
PARENT EDITION

DR. ROBYN REU GRAHAM

EDITED BY
DEBORAH KEVIN

HIGHLANDER
PRESS

YOU, ME, AND ANXIETY: PARENT EDITION.
Copyright © 2022 by Dr. Robyn Reu Graham

All rights reserved. The contents of this book may not be transmitted or reproduced in any form or by any means, mechanical or electronic, including photocopying, recording or by any information storage and retrieval system, without prior written permission from the author, with the exception only of the inclusion of brief quotations in a review.

Limit of Liability Disclaimer: The contents of this book are intended for information purposes only and may not apply to your individual situation. The author, publisher, and distributor in no way guarantee the accuracy of the contents. The information is subjective and should be treated as such when reviewing the contents. Neither the Publisher nor the author shall be liable for any loss of profit or any other commercial damages resulting from actions taken based on the contents of this guide. All links contained in this book are for information purposes only and are not warranted for content, accuracy, or any other implied or explicit purpose.

ISBN: 978-1-956442-00-7
Ebook ISBN: 978-1-956442-01-4
Library of Congress Control Number: Applied for.

Published by Highlander Press
501 W. University Pkwy, Ste. B2
Baltimore, MD 21210

Cover design: Christy Collins/Constellation Book Services
Front cover image: imnoom, www.istockphoto.com
Editor: Deborah Kevin, MA
Author's photo credit: Aliza Schlabach

Printed in the United States of America

*For my family: John, Joshua, Samuel, and Grace.
My source of life. My joy. My heart.*

Contents

Foreword Tamra Andress	xvii
How To Use This Book	xxi
Introduction	xxiii
1. Be the Hero	1
2. Anxiety	11
3. Anger	29
4. Shame	41
5. Fear	47
6. Image	59
7. Relationships	69
8. Laughter	95
9. Kindness	99
10. Apologies	101
11. Trust	107
12. Faith	113
13. Values	125
14. Perfection	131
15. Comparison	135
16. Grace	139
17. Curiosity	143
18. Hope	147
19. Self-discipline, Intentions, and Creating Healthy Habits	149
20. Confidence	153
21. Gratitude	157
22. The 5Cs Journaling Method	161
23. Intentional Actions for Overcoming Anxiety	165
24. Conclusion	179
Bible Verses Toolkit	183

Resources	187
References	189
Acknowledgments	193
About the Author	197
About the Publisher	199

Foreword

TAMRA ANDRESS

The moment we are born, we start exploring the world. We investigate light and colors. We tune in to sounds, like the voice of our mama or the woo of our own coo. We dissect tastes and texture and define likes and dislikes accordingly. (Side note: I had a strange fixation with Gerber jarred baby food into my adolescent years. Don't ask and remember this is a judgement free zone.)

Since our birth, not only are we analyzing the inputs, we are also being taught about them intentionally with hopes of our understanding of this space and place in which we inhabit. As the journey to existence continues and we start to "grow up," we start to sense a separation between what's happening around us compared to what's happening within us. As a society, we are so prone and fixated on the exterior, that we (ourselves and our parents too) often forget, because we aren't ever taught, the key critical component of looking within to explore ourselves.

Emotional intelligence (EQ) is like your IQ. If IQ is your knowledge container for understanding information you've learned, then EQ is your feelings container both learned and innate. I didn't learn about this until I was into my thirties and dealing with anxiety for the first time in my life.

I would wake up with full body shakes from nightmares and not be able to go back to sleep. I'd get new information about a relationship or situation and it would seemingly halt my ability to process, function or create anything other than fog, exhaustion and oftentimes tears.

As I began exploring what was happening to my mind and body, I was introduced to the concept of fight, flight, freeze, and faint connected to my EQ. We all have a reticular activating system, which Dr. Graham gets into later, that is working to protect us and keep us safe. However, environmental factors and learned lessons can sometimes trick us into a response that isn't necessarily true. This is the concept of a limiting belief.

And I can tell you, fellow warrior, you are capable of understanding and overcoming the current state and struggle against yourself or what you may be witnessing with the child(ren) you love.

It was months in before I comprehended what fully was transpiring and even a couple years before I had language and ability to counteract the emotions from triggers.

This human existence thing is a wild ride, isn't it? We all experience highs, lows and in-betweens, and unfortunately anxiety often keeps us trapped in the lows. My hope, since you've taken the effort to pick up this essential handbook, is that you are willing to invest enough to move past the darkness of the lows [that can control and stifle us] into the enjoyment of the in-betweens and the greatest memories of your life.

You may have seen the popular Pixar movie, *Inside Out*. If not, I highly suggest preparing some air-pop popcorn to sit down, listen, and learn. The film maker, Pete Docter, created this representation of life as he witnessed the shift of his daughter from playful child to grim adolescent. This movie explores the mind and helps to answer the critical question, "What are you thinking?" No matter on which side of the coin we fall (the one experiencing anxiety internally or the one supporting the person with it), we're all wondering the same thing. This book will help give you those answers.

The movie depicts emotions beautifully and makes light to the recognition that even the feelings we have been programmed to assume are "bad" or "negative" all have a place and purpose within us. And, therefore, since God was intentional with His 'good' design (reference

Genesis 1:31) no part of us is "bad." We can use all things, even feelings like anxiety, to help guide and teach us something new about ourselves that we can learn to appreciate and love. Our EQ helps us operate with everyone else as we become aware of our inside world, environment and how we relate to others simultaneously.

After reading Dr. Graham's book, I believe you will have fresh breath and perspective to each of these Pixar characters that make up your personal everyday adventure. And it will also help deplete the depths of worry that can be associated to living a life filled with anxiety.

My last bit of encouragement, before you start dissecting Dr. Graham's wisdom, is that you follow her guidance on using this as a tool book and resource guide to navigate and truly activate the lessons learned. Her dual-sided understanding of anxiety gives her a unique lens to build perspective and appreciation for the God within us all, no matter what we might be thinking or feeling.

You are not crazy. You are crazy awesome. Now let's start exploring ourselves from the inside out instead of the outside in.

How To Use This Book

This book is not meant to diagnose or treat anxiety, or to take the place of clinical intervention with a healthcare provider.

I originally wrote *You, Me, and Anxiety* **with teen girls in mind**. However, I decided that for the book to provide the most value, I needed to include information for parents. Overcoming anxiety is a team effort; no one can do it alone.

TEENS

As you read this book, you will find examples of activities that I encourage you to do. You can find all activities in the accompanying journal. To get the most out of the book and the best results as you navigate life with anxiety, take the time to do the activities and exercises.

PARENTS

After each chapter, I have included a parent section. Please read the teen and parent sections to give you a better perspective about living with a teen with anxiety. My hope is that this book will help you parent your child with anxiety while maintaining peace in your home. As you read, you may discover that you have symptoms of anxiety as well, without ever being diagnosed or knowing what you were experiencing. If this happens, I encourage you to do the exercises in the journal too. Although this book is written for teen girls, I believe it has the potential to help anyone who is living with anxiety.

Note, I put the parent section at the end of each teen section because I speak to the teen section in the parent sections. However, if you would like to dive into the parent section prior to reading the teen section, you still will be able to make sense of each chapter. *You, Me, and Anxiety* is meant to be a guide for you and your teen. Use the book in the way that works best for you and your circumstances.

Introduction

You are not alone.

Whether you're a teen moving through the challenges of anxiety or a parent trying to help your child navigate their experiences, you are not alone.

Over twenty-five percent of children between the ages of thirteen and eighteen have anxiety disorders. Anxiety affects over eighteen percent of the U.S. population and is the most common cause of mental illness. Anxiety disorders can be equally as disabling as other mental health diagnoses but does not receive the same recognition. Some of the effects of anxiety include decreased productivity, increased morbidity and mortality, eating disorders, and increased substance abuse. The lifetime prevalence of anxiety is especially high in teens and is more prevalent in girls than boys, but boys are not immune.

Who am I to speak to this? I am Robyn, a little girl, teenager, college student, woman, wife, mom, sister, and friend who has lived her entire life fighting with the demons of anxiety, missing out on wonderful experiences and meaningful relationships because I let anxiety rule my thoughts.

With my history of anxiety, having watched my son suffer from anxiety, and having watched numerous family members, friends, and the children of friends suffer from anxiety, I have set out to help people recognize anxiety as a disease that should be respected just as diabetes, asthma, heart disease, or cancer are respected. Mental health challenges are often hidden by patients and families due to fears of being stereotyped or judged by others. It is time for society to recognize anxiety as an illness. If not addressed and treated, the result can be frighteningly dramatic, such as suicide. Death is too great a price to pay for something that is treatable. Alarmingly, even though anxiety disorders are highly treatable, only 36.9 percent of people suffering with anxiety receive treatment. Some may question whether I have the expertise to write this book. Am I a psychiatrist? No. Am I a therapist who treats anxiety disorders? No. Am I a researcher in mental health? No. I'm not a physician, psychiatrist, or a therapist. My expertise lies in having lived with generalized and social anxiety disorder my whole life and supporting my son through his journey with social anxiety. I witnessed my father suffer through anxiety (only we didn't know what it was while we were growing up). So, I've seen it from all sides, and it's from this place of wisdom that I offer insight and guidance. In addition to my life experiences, I have researched for papers and projects in pharmacy school, and as a consultant and medical writer.

I am a woman who happens to have a doctorate in pharmacy and has lived with anxiety and its impact for my entire life. I've experienced and witnessed the physical and emotional impacts anxiety has on people, adults, children, and teens, and on their relationships with themselves and others. A degree or specialty title is not necessary to increase the awareness and depths of effects that anxiety can have on individuals and society. Anxiety can be debilitating. It can result in the inability to build and maintain relationships, prevent people from having productive, happy lives, and causes people to hide in shame and sadness. Plus, it prevents people from living the life God called them to live.

When the concept of this book originated, I thought it would be based on my gifts as a photographer, envisioning a book filled with pictures of individuals depicting their anxiety. Children and teens would use the book to identify and describe their own feelings without having to put words to them. However, as I prayed about this project,

INTRODUCTION

God led me to not only share photographs, but to provide a more meaningful journey into anxiety, living a purposeful and meaningful life with scripture and God's love as another pillar to lean on. As I write this book and think of future readers, I want to leave you with the blessing of confidence, grace, courage, faith, and love.

Feel confident that you are a child of God and He made you the way you are because He has a plan for you.

Give yourself grace to accept who you are and be kind to yourself. Realize your worth and advocate for yourself.

Have courage to face each day with strength and perseverance, and never give up the fight to get the help you need and live the life you dream of. Leave the doubts and denial of self-worth on the path behind you, and look only forward to a positive, meaningful future of purpose.

Depend on faith in God and in yourself, that through Him and the will He gave you, you will have the strength to face anxiety with courage. Have faith that you will find deeper meaning for what you are going through, have gone through, or will go through on your life journey.

Love yourself. It is important to love yourself before you try or are able to love and care for others. You are lovable and worthy of love. God has proven that through His gift of grace.

It is my hope that through your journey with this book, you will be able to shift your mindset around anxiety. Mindset is eighty to ninety-five percent of what makes us successful in life. No matter your skill sets, a positive mindset is super important to be able to take action and for that action to be effective. The exercises within the chapters will guide and help you to build habits that will lead to a positive mindset. Don't just read about them, do them. Action is powerful.

Be the Hero

Hero:// a person admired for achievements and noble qualities; one who shows great courage

YOU ARE the hero of your journey. Being your own hero doesn't mean to go through life alone, or you do it all by yourself. It is about embracing courage and taking one intentional action after another to get to where you want to be, emotionally, physically, and spiritually. Being your own hero is about making decisions to always do the next right thing. To seek help when help is needed and to give help when the opportunity arises. You can be a hero by simply recognizing that you need help. Your journey of being your own hero begins today as you read the pages of this book.

There may be days that you don't want to get out of bed, don't even want to pick up this book or do the activities I've included, but that doesn't mean you aren't a hero. A hero is someone who makes a choice to be better, to do better, to do the next right thing, to do the things that seem the absolute hardest, and today, you are that someone.

Let's dive into how together we can raise our heads and hearts as heroes and win the fight with anxiety.

Sometimes, maybe even often, people have symptoms of anxiety but don't recognize them as such. Anxiety disorders present in different ways for each one of us. I have always had physical symptoms of anxiety. Quite often the physical symptoms present before I realize I am anxious. And, sometimes, my mind just won't be quiet.

Often, we experience the symptoms or thoughts listed below, and go to the doctor just for her to tell us there is nothing wrong. She can't find any physical reason for what we are feeling or experiencing. Not having a diagnosis handed to us can be very frustrating and overwhelming. The more there are no clinical findings for what we are feeling and experiencing, the more we think we are making this up, that it's not real, and we begin to feel crazy.

Have any of these phrases rolled across your tongue or swirled around in your mind? Does your heart race at the thought of going to a party? Does your stomach hurt when it's time to go to school? Have you been to the doctor, but she can't find anything wrong with you despite a myriad of tests? If yes, anxiety could be influencing your daily life.

Below is a list of physical symptoms and thoughts that you might be experiencing that may indicate you have a form of anxiety:

- My stomach hurts.
- My head always hurts.
- I don't feel good.
- I am not good enough.
- I can't.
- No one gets me.
- I am fat.
- I am ugly.
- My heart races.
- I'm afraid to.
- I can't breathe.
- My chest is tight.
- I hate myself.
- I can't get out of bed.
- My body hurts.
- I'm so tired.

- I can't sleep.
- I feel angry all the time.
- I'm irritable.
- I'm jumpy
- I can't focus.
- My mind is racing.
- I can't quiet my thoughts.
- My thoughts are all over the place.
- I'm scared all the time.
- I worry all the time.
- I never just have fun.
- I'm stupid.
- I'm dumb.
- Dark or negative thoughts (comments)
- Sharing dark or negative things on social media.
- Putting yourself down.
- Feeling a sense of despair and deep sadness.
- Injuring yourself or inflicting pain on yourself.
- Hurting others verbally or physically.

I want to remind you that you are not alone. Anxiety, especially in teens, is growing in prevalence. Even more importantly, I want you to realize that you have options for help. You do not have to go through anxiety alone.

One of the first steps you can take is to be honest with yourself, and your parents and/or guidance counselor at school. If you are experiencing any of the above thoughts or feelings, chances are you could use help navigating the struggle with anxiety.

Pay attention to your symptoms. When do they occur? What is happening in your life when you experience the symptoms? Notice triggers, such as school, tests, peers, going to new places, doing a presentation, deadlines, social events, or your parents arguing.

We all have certain things that make us more anxious than others. When I have something big coming up, like a presentation, trip, or major decision, my stomach hurts. I feel like I am getting sick with a stomach bug. I may go a couple of days with my stomach feeling this way before I realize I am anxious about something. Once I dissect what is happening in my life, I realize what I am anxious about. Then, I can work on my thoughts and calm the physical symptoms as well as the emotions.

I catch the anxious or negative thoughts, I challenge them, and then I can change them. Years ago, a wonderful therapist taught me about cognitive behavioral therapy and gave me the method of catch, challenge, and change my thoughts. I added control and confidence to it to begin using the 5Cs journaling method:

1. Catch the thoughts.
2. Challenge the thoughts.
3. Change the thoughts.
4. Control the thoughts and feelings
5. Confidence that catapults you forward.

However, before you can catch the thoughts, you must be aware of the symptoms accompanying them.

Let's take a deeper dive into the 5Cs journaling method.

CATCH

Once you begin to recognize the thoughts and feelings associated with your anxiety, which may take some time, you will start to recognize them sooner than later. Once you recognize them, it's time to write them down so you can work around them. By work I mean now that we caught the thoughts, we are going to challenge them.

CHALLENGE

You know in school when a teacher adds a bonus question to a test for extra credit? The teacher is challenging you to pull additional knowledge out of your brain bank, and if you can, you are rewarded with extra credit points and a higher grade.

It's similar when challenging your thoughts. You have to dig deep into your brain bank to evaluate whether or not the thoughts make sense and are legitimate. You use past experiences to do this. As you remember times you made it through a situation or experience, you can counteract the negative thoughts by telling yourself you've already done this, and it will be okay. Once you challenge the negative thoughts by questioning their validity, you can begin working to change them.

CHANGE

Changing the thoughts brings the reward of extra credit points in the form of feeling better and happier. Changing the thoughts begins with challenging them. As you look at the positive experiences and thoughts and begin to shift the focus from the negative to the positive, you will begin to feel better and have a more positive outlook on the experience you are anxious about.

CONTROL AND CONFIDENCE

The more you do these exercises, the better you will be able to control your thoughts when future experiences trigger anxious thoughts. As you gain more control over your thoughts, you will begin to feel more confident. As confidence builds, you'll find yourself able to catapult yourself into cycles of more positive thoughts. You'll try new experiences, go new places, perhaps focus and sleep better, and build relationships with more ease.

Each C leads to the next. Eventually, practicing them will help you get to the point where you are able to alleviate the symptoms of anxiety closer to the onset of them, instead of suffering through them for longer periods of time.

The most important thing to take away from this book is that you can live a meaningful, purposeful, and positive life if you invest the time to get a grip on anxiety now. The shift won't happen overnight, and at times, it may be hard for you. Some days it may feel like work. Know that if you are willing to invest in yourself now, your efforts will pay off, and you can live a life without regret or too many disappointments.

The journey to overcome anxiety is one that has been never ending for me. I don't tell you that to discourage you. I constantly remind myself to implement the 5Cs journaling method. If I don't, the anxiety will consume how I live each day. Sometimes, this happens because we have so many external influences, especially with social media. It is easy to get distracted and compare ourselves to others. I have to catch my anxious thoughts and do work around the what ifs to quiet my mind. Thankfully, now I have the tools to help me in a timely manner, and do not have to live in the depths of anxiety and its symptoms every day.

Anxiety can hold you back. It can prevent you from following the path that leads to fulfillment, joy, purpose, and healthy relationships.

It wasn't until I was in my late thirties that I finally invested the necessary time to understand what was happening, why I did what I did, why I felt the way I felt, why I behaved the way I did, and why I made the decisions I made. That's when I learned the 5Cs journaling method and really changed my life for the better. I started living the way I wanted to live, not letting anxiety dictate how I spent my time and how I felt.

I do not want you to live like I did. I want you to live each day making decisions that you will never regret. I want you to cherish the opportunities, moments, and relationships that come and go throughout your life. I missed out on a lot over the years. Anxiety kept me afraid to try new things. It kept me from doing things and having cool experiences with my peers. Anxiety held me back.

All the experiences and relationships you have or do not have now will influence your adult life, and your ability to live in the moment, to live deeply passionate, purposeful and joyful lives.

It's time to make the decision that you want to be the author of your story. You want to be your own hero. It's a role that only you can play while writing the story of your life.

I had to humble myself and ask for help. Fear held me back for a long time. I didn't want anyone to know I was struggling emotionally. What would they think of me? Maybe they wouldn't want to be my friend. What if there was really something wrong with me?

Thank goodness I finally took steps to becoming my own hero. I intentionally sought out a therapist who could help me take action to change my life. I wanted to change, to become the hero of my own journey. I didn't do it alone. I had the support of my husband, my therapist, and God. Collectively, we created a hero in me—one that could face situations, problems, challenges, and people, without getting sick or letting fear hold me back in a river of misery.

So here I am, sharing my story alongside advice that I've discovered worked for me. I want to help you to continue to grow as the hero of your journey with anxiety.

But, before we take this journey together, I want to emphasize that asking for help doesn't mean you are weak, it means you are brave and taking action over anxiety.

I think you will be surprised at the love you will receive when you open your arms to help. To move through this journey with an open mind, do this exercise.

> Sit quietly. Open your arms and think of help coming into you. Now pull that help into your heart. Then reach out and welcome more. Bring it into your heart too. Repeat until you feel ready to accept the help and love you are so very worthy of.

> Humble yourselves, therefore, under God's mighty hand, that he may lift you up in due time. Cast all your anxiety on him because he cares for you.
>
> 1 PETER 5:6-7

PARENTS

In many ways I am certain you are already perceived as a hero to your child(ren). After all, you were their first love, the one who cares for and provides for them, and the one who has always had the solution to their problems. Even through a journey with anxiety, you will remain their hero, but there will be days that neither you nor they will think so.

Navigating days with anxiety can leave you feeling exhausted, overwhelmed, and sad. I think the hardest thing in life is watching your child go through an experience in which you have no control over. There will be days when you think you have no control over their anxiety or how they behave toward you or others. Here's the reality: Being there for them, recognizing their struggles, educating yourself (reading this book for starters), and getting them the help they need will be the best ways to have some control.

When dealing with anxiety, take one day at a time. This may seem dramatic, but having lived through it, it's a reality. One day everything is great. Progress has been made, and there are no outbursts or tears. But the next day is ten times worse than the incident last week. Things will come at you out of the blue, and you'll find yourself walking on eggshells. Therefore, patience, grace, and self-care will become so important in your daily life. You will need a break from your child(ren) with anxiety, and they will need a break from you. Therapy may be that break. Setting aside time for a workout, or simply following a routine, may also serve as ways to keep yourself and your child in a state of (pseudo) balance.

The other area of your life you will need to take special care for is your relationship with your spouse, or the child(ren)'s other parent. If married, having a child with anxiety can take a toll on your relationship. To preserve your marriage, it will be important to have difficult conversations about having consistent parenting practices. This becomes especially challenging when one parent has anxiety, and the other does not. People who have not lived with anxiety can get extremely frustrated with a child who has anxiety. If one parent has anxiety, the one who doesn't may pass blame (unjustifiably). There is a great need for the two of you to come to an agreement about how you help the child(ren) and what you discuss in front of them. Your disagreements about anxiety, or your child(ren), will only make your child(ren) more anxious.

Case in point: My husband has never had anxiety. He has always been able to speak professionally to any size group, never was afraid of public speaking, and has never had any type of paralyzing anxiety. When our son experienced an inability to speak in front of his class, the teacher was kind and suggested he practice at home and do the presentation for us. If he could do so, she would give him a good grade because he had done all the work necessary to prepare and do a great job. I completely understood what he was going through. I had experienced it. My husband could not understand his inability to present in front of us at all. The situation ended up with my husband raising his voice at our son saying, "just do it," and my screaming at him that he couldn't talk to our son that way and that he didn't understand what our son was going through. He finally understood and once calm had been restored, we were able to work through the situation with our son together.

I am not telling you this story to throw my husband under the bus, but from that day forward, we had boundaries with how issues related to anxiety were handled. And, we were able to survive, and our son was able to thrive.

As with everything in life, it takes teamwork to make the dream work. Our dream was to have happy, healthy children. To achieve that we had to work together, and each take on the responsibilities that we were most capable of. Did we do everything right? No, not at all. But I think that looking back, our son would still say we are his heroes, in totally different ways, and we were always there to champion him. We did so in different ways and were each the "go to" for different types of circumstances.

I can assure you neither of us are perfect. Over the years we've both had to teach the other things for us to be able to work together. Communication has been the key.

Anxiety

Anxiety:// an abnormal and overwhelming sense of apprehension and fear often marked by physical signs (such as tension, sweating, and increased pulse rate), by doubt concerning the reality and nature of the threat, and by self-doubt about one's capacity to cope with it.

 Every moment is a fresh beginning.

T. S. ELIOT

THROUGHOUT THE FOLLOWING CHAPTERS, I will share my opinions. Some of my opinions are based on scientific data, while some are based on my life experiences and beliefs. Please keep this in perspective. This book is meant to guide you to find peace and live without overwhelming anxiety, so you can find times of complete joy, discover life, and build positive relationships with yourself and others.

NERVOUS VERSUS ANXIOUS

Let's start with the difference between being nervous and feeling anxious. People who do not suffer from anxiety often say things like "oh, you don't have to be nervous," or "don't be so nervous; it's not a big deal," or "why are you so nervous?" Has anyone said these things to you before? I know I've heard them.

There is a difference in the two: One can be navigated with ease and the other can be prohibitive and stifling.

Nervous, to me, means feeling excited yet a little afraid, usually right before an event or circumstance. Being nervous doesn't have long-lasting effects. The palms of my hands may sweat, or I may feel a little jittery or have to pee, but that is the extent of it. Once the event or circumstance is over, the nervousness ends.

Anxiety, on the other hand, may result in physical symptoms and potentially the inability to do something. For example, you may feel stomachaches, headaches, tight or sore muscles, an inability to sleep, or your mind feels like it's exploding with "what if" thoughts. With anxiety, it is difficult to focus. The mind races about the impending event, a person, or situation. The "symptoms" don't stop once the event or experience passes. The mind continues to race and ponder the "what ifs."

Here is an example: Some people may get nervous before a test. Some people have significant test anxiety. I fall into the later. Sure, my grades were always good; I was a great student and worked really hard. But, when it came to taking a timed test, I panicked. When I was in elementary and middle grades, we had timed reading tests. We read a pamphlet and then answered questions about the content. I was so focused on being timed (and I was a slow reader), I panicked. I often had to miss recess to do the reading tests because I was not able to finish them during the normal time frame.

Reading aloud in class was another major source of anxiety. I didn't hear or learn from what anyone else read because I was reading ahead to practice what I might have to read aloud. My voice would quiver as I read. My stomach hurt, and I wanted to cry.

This didn't make sense. I may have been a slow reader, but I was an avid, good reader. Anxiety had me so worked up about reading aloud, I missed classwork and had to do more work after school to catch up.

Another example of test anxiety is the ACT exams. I am so happy that many universities and colleges are doing away with test requirements. I was physically sick before I was scheduled to take the ACT exam. In fact, my mother and I didn't think I would be able to take it. My mother called my French teacher to come talk to me and convince me that I could take the exam.

To this day, I remember the classroom I was in: old wooden and metal desks with wooden and metal chairs, greenish blue colored walls, a huge chalk board across the front of the room. I sat at the first desk in a row of five, and the clock was right in front of me. I was so anxious. I wanted to cry the entire time. The clock was an eminent ticking time bomb.

When I finished, I felt as though I could collapse. But it was behind me. Unsurprisingly, I only scored an eighteen—barely high enough to get me into college, but not high enough for me to get into pharmacy school, the only school I was applying to.

My poor mother. She didn't tell me this. She told me that there was a scholarship test and I needed to sit for it. She took me to the college, and I sat for the exam. I knew I wasn't going to get a scholarship (those negative anxious thoughts speaking) and so I took the test with much less anxiety. After the fact, when we received the results of the exam and I was accepted to pharmacy school, my mother came clean. It had indeed been a scholarship test for most of the students present, but for me and a few select others who wanted to become pharmacists but didn't have high enough ACT scores, we were there to prove ourselves.

To this day I am grateful my mother didn't tell me. I can't even imagine the pressure.

GET OVER IT

Let's begin by making the decision that you won't accept the words "get over it" from an outsider. People who say those words to you might not understand what is happening inside of your mind, heart, or body. When someone says, "get over it," you may assume that means they think that you are acting like a baby, being dramatic, or that they are annoyed and don't want to deal with your emotional swings anymore.

It is possible that your thoughts are true, but you don't know for sure what anyone else is thinking. I think it's safe to think that people who say "get over it" may not understand you because they don't understand anxiety. You haven't shared all of your thoughts and feelings with them, so they may not understand why you are acting the way you are acting or saying and doing the things you are saying and doing. As humans we all want everything and everyone to be "normal." But what is normal? Normal to you may be different than normal to me. Another person's opinion of normal is what they may be expecting from you, especially if they aren't aware of what you are going through.

When people don't behave in ways we expect or want them to, it can be overwhelming and frustrating. If someone makes you feel like they don't care about you, especially if they say, "just get over it", remember they probably have an idea of how they think things should be, and aren't sure how to react to you or your behaviors.

Maybe people are coming from a place of judgement when they say, "get over it," but I think we have to give them the benefit of the doubt that it may just be a lack of understanding. It then becomes your job to explain how you are feeling and what is happening inside of you so they can begin to understand and maybe even begin to help you.

In the previous chapter, I wrote about the 5Cs journaling method. They seem simple, right? However, they may not be. How you respond to activating the 5Cs journaling method will be specific to you and your journey with anxiety.

Anxiety can be genetic, or it can be the result of trauma, environmental factors, or a life experience (think Post Traumatic Stress Disorder or PTSD). It could have been with you all your life but was dormant and symptoms didn't appear until just recently. Whatever the cause of your anxiety, it will take time to retrain your mind to redirect your thoughts. It's quite possible you will see positive changes quickly, but I urge you to be patient for long-term effects. The mind is an amazing, complex thing, and you may have a good day using the 5Cs journaling method but then a few bad days where you have to put in the work to retrain the thoughts again. Be patient. The more you do the work, the better you will feel over time.

Take time to look back at your life and notice how you felt and the decisions you made about experiences, circumstances, and relationships. Are there times in which you:

- Regret the decision you made;
- Missed out on something fun;
- Pulled away from a friend;
- Didn't feel good enough to participate in something;
- Felt like you didn't fit in;
- Had a fight with someone;
- Freaked out for no apparent reason;
- Felt super angry but didn't know why;
- Were too afraid to do something that you knew would be fun; or
- Didn't do something because you were afraid something bad would happen?

Here's an exercise you can do to determine how different experiences affect you physically. On the left, write down an experience that made you feel anxious. On the right, right down how it felt in your body.

What Was the Experience?	How Did I Physically Feel?
Trying out for the basketball team	Sick to my stomach
Asked to do a solo at the band concert	Headache, shaky, stomach pains
Packing for vacation	Tired, unable to focus
Didn't go to a party with a friend	Cried, exhausted, shaky, threw up

Do you see a pattern? Were there similar circumstances that you felt the same way about? Were there certain people involved with various experiences? Did you have the same physical symptoms around multiple scenarios that prevented you from having these experiences? Was it a feeling of fear that held you back from each experience? Did you repeatedly react inappropriately to situations? If you had similar reactions, physically or emotionally, to a number of situations, you could start to break down how anxiety is causing you to react and influencing the decisions you make.

Many times, there are behaviors or symptoms associated with anxiety that we don't even realize. When making a list, we may be able to begin to recognize what the symptoms are so that we are more aware going forward and don't continually repeat the same behaviors. Implementing a strategy like the 5Cs journaling method may help you stop any negative emotional reactions or consistent negative reactions or behaviors.

For example, when I have to do a presentation, my stomach will hurt. The pain is real. I also get irritable and easily frustrated with others. The presentation could be a month away, but I am having these symptoms. It's the flight or fight mechanism going on in my brain without me even realizing it. Then I will catch myself trying to come up with excuses as to why I can't do the presentation.

In the past, my reaction to speaking was a vicious cycle. It was debilitating. It took joy from me and changed the course of my life.

Fortunately for me, I have been able to overcome the anxiety associated with public speaking, and life worked out alright. However, I was left with disappointment, and I lost years in my career and ultimately went a different direction in my life than I had originally planned.

Here's my story, and it's one I don't want you to follow:

I was working on my doctorate degree. Hard work was part of my core being, and I always had a drive to succeed. Yes, I wanted to succeed and do well for myself, but I also spent way too much time worried about what others thought about me or whether I was good enough. It was a miserable existence because I couldn't live in the moment and just go with the flow.

Part of my doctorate project, similar to a thesis, was to conduct a study with a faculty advisor and do a presentation on it. The study was months long and a subject I loved and was interested in. Oncology and immunology were interests of mine at the time. I worked at Jewish Hospital as a pharmacy student and was fortunate that my faculty advisor worked in the clinical pharmacy department. He was the nicest guy and super smart.

Together, we designed the study. Please forgive me if I don't remember all the details around the design, but we collected data on how patients responded to Granulocyte Colony-Stimulating Factor (G-CSF). G-CSF stimulates bone marrow to make granulocytes (white blood cells) and stem cells, which are needed for cancer patients undergoing chemotherapy to prevent infection or fevers caused by chemotherapy.

G-CSF was relatively new to the market and very expensive. We wanted to determine the cost-effectiveness of G-CSF. We wanted to document whether patients undergoing chemotherapy had fewer infections and fever episodes when receiving G-CSF therapy.

I was, and still am, a total geek about things like this. As I write this, I want to dive back into the clinical side of pharmacy and research.

Anyway, once the project was complete, I was to present the project to the faculty and other doctorate students in the program. I don't remember the exact time frame, but the project spanned at least six months. I did the work and invested much time and energy into the project, while going to school and working part-time. It was not an easy schedule, but it was one that I was accustomed to; the grit and grind was just part of reaching my goals to obtain the degree.

I have always had a love of learning and working hard so I was thriving. Until I wasn't Collecting the data, evaluating it, and creating a PowerPoint presentation were the easy parts. When it came time to present the project, I became overwhelmed and frozen with anxiety. I didn't want to tell my advisor. What would he think of me?

Instead of seeking help and guidance, presentation strategies, and moral support, I quit! I was going to be Dr. Robyn Reu, and I walked away because I couldn't do a presentation. At that moment, I believed with my whole being that I couldn't do it.

I knew the data. I knew everyone who would be in the room when I was presenting. There was no reason I was so overcome with fear that I couldn't do the presentation, except for the fact that I suffered from severe anxiety. The anxious thoughts took over my reality and my ability to reason with myself. Had I just done the presentation, I might have gotten a C on it. I wouldn't have failed, and I probably would have had an A on the actual study. The grade would have averaged out fine. It might not have been perfect, but it would have been done, and I would have had my doctorate degree in my hand at the same time my best friends did. But I couldn't do it.

I am fortunate that God redirected my path. I went to work using my B.S. degree as a pharmacist for a year or so and then went back to school. I had to do another project, but I was all in and committed.

This time I dove into data on hypercholesterolemia drugs. I collected data on cholesterol-lowering agents and their cost efficacy. My new faculty advisor (who was equally as nice as the first one) and I designed the study to observe how effective different doses of the cholesterol-lowering drugs were, and whether or not patients had side effects or decreased incidence of heart attacks while taking the drugs.

It was okay. It wasn't as interesting, and the charts were extensive to review. But I did the project, and I did the presentation and graduated with that doctorate in hand.
I wasn't going to walk for graduation. I was embarrassed that I had quit and come back. However, my father and mother

convinced me to do it, so I did. There are so many cool parts of this story, but here are a few of my favorites.

1. My daddy was in the front row of the auditorium when I gave the presentation. I couldn't have asked for better moral support.
2. I didn't know it at the time, but my future husband and father to my children was in the auditorium to evaluate my presentation.
3. Years later, when my father was dying of cancer, I was upstairs in my old bedroom packing to return home. My daddy knew how sad I was to leave, and he climbed the stairs to talk to me, just the two of us. He gave me a hug and said to me, "The proudest moment of my life was when you crossed that stage with a doctorate degree."

Not everyone is as fortunate as I am. I already had a degree, so no matter what, I could work and have a successful life and make a good salary. Many people, though, fall victim to anxiety and lose more than a year or two of the life they worked hard to achieve.

Why do I tell you this story? Because every decision you make is empowering, either for or against what your goals are. Understand that anxiety can take control of your mind, but you do not have to submit to that control. You are strong, you are capable, and you do not have to quit. If you look at the entire experience, you can learn to navigate the anxiety, and instead of letting it debilitate you, use it to push your forward to be the best you can be.

When I did the presentation the second time around, I got a B. It wasn't perfect, but nothing and no one ever is. I was a nervous wreck, but I made the conscious decision that I wanted that degree, and I was not going to let that presentation deter me again. I learned there is no such thing as perfection. But we can be satisfied and proud if we know, in our hearts, we did our best and that we achieved something we previously didn't think was possible.

I think it is also worth mentioning that if you need a break from something because physically, emotionally, or mentally you just can't push through, that is fine too. Each of us has a unique set of circumstances and need to handle the situation the way that is best for us. The important thing is when you step away, commit to it being temporary and do not give up on the dream or goal you had set out to achieve.

OUR THOUGHTS CREATE OUR RESULTS

This is a powerful statement to remember. Thoughts of worry have the potential to hold you back. They may even cause bad things to happen. When you recognize thoughts of worry, fear, or doubt, catch them and change them to something positive. No what ifs about something negative happening. Rephrase those thoughts to positive what ifs. Instead of, "what if I fail" change it to "what if I get an A."

If I hadn't changed my mindset and thoughts around doing the presentation for my doctorate, I would never have achieved my goal. It wasn't easy to recognize that I was holding myself back and letting anxiety control me. But, once I made the decision to refocus my mental energy, I was able to do what I wanted and needed to do to get the degree.

NEGATIVITY BIAS

Did you know that your amygdala (a part of your brain) is like an alarm clock for negative experiences or negative emotional feedback? The neurons in the amygdala will look for negative or bad things two-thirds more often than positive. These negative thoughts and experiences are then woven into your brain, leaving a permanent implant that your brain will reference time and time again. This happens in seconds, whereas positive experiences can take twelve seconds or more to be permanently stored in the brain. Negative experiences also stay in the brain much longer than positive experiences. Scientifically, there is an asymmetry in how the brain processes and remembers negative and positive experiences. This is called negativity bias.

Knowing how the brain works makes it easier to understand how having negative conversations with yourself can influence your perspective of success and inhibit your ability to overcome anxiety. If you say the following things to yourself, they will be woven into the fibers of your brain and believed:

- I am not smart.
- I am fat.
- I am ugly.
- I don't have any friends.
- I'm stupid.
- I'm boring.
- I'm slow.
- I can't learn.
- I'm weird.

These sayings, especially if said repeatedly, become part of your existence and the longer this happens, the harder it will be to reverse the thoughts. Compare those statements to the following positive phrases:

- I am capable.
- I am unique.
- I am happy.
- I can do it.
- I'm pretty.
- I'm fit.
- I may not be fast but I'm not slow.
- I may not be at the top of the class, but I work hard and get good grades.
- My body does exactly what I need it to.
- I'm healthy.

Now that you know that every negative thought you have even, if not said out loud, will bring you down and hold you back because it is stuck in your brain, you can begin to recognize these thoughts immediately and change them quickly. Changing the negative thoughts quickly or avoiding them all together will help save time and energy in the future.

I didn't have this luxury until recent years. And I can assure you:

Those negative thoughts were near permanent impressions in my brain. It has taken me a very long time to change that dialogue in my mind.

DON'T RUSH

Anxiety and worry can often lead us to want to speed time along—to rush through circumstances and situations. We often rush from one thought to the other, from one what if to another what if.

Have you ever felt so anxious about something that you just wanted it over with? I have, many times. It may have been a speaking engagement that I was dreading, a trip I was taking, or some other event like a party or gala.

I used to spend so much time worrying about what to wear and what to say, going over so many what ifs in my mind that I was miserable and wished time away. I just wanted whatever it was to be over with. Sadly, I can't get any of that time I wished away returned to me. And, you know what? The party, the event, the speaking engagement went well. I rocked the speech, I had a ton of fun at the event, or the time went way too quickly on the trip, and I found myself wishing for more time.

Instead of rushing from one thought to another or wishing time away because I wanted to avoid something, I now use my 5Cs journaling method strategy to stay focused on the moment, the task at hand and the people around me, and I don't let the anxiety ruin the preparation period.

I'm not going to say I don't have the what if thoughts, I do. But I now know how to manage them, and I have learned that most of them are silly and not realistic at all.

In fact, I have actually shown up to events in the "wrong" outfit, and you know what? The what ifs around what to wear didn't come true. Nothing bad happened. What it took me so long to realize is that every situation is manageable. Nothing detrimental has happened and most likely won't happen. The key is in how I, or you, choose to handle it. Laugh it off and roll with it, or panic and let the situation fuel anxiety for future scenarios.

As you will see throughout the next few chapters, you have to work hard to navigate or overcome anxiety. If we rush through the process, we won't be able to maintain the reduced level of anxiety long-term.

Patience is a virtue. Ahhhh, but it can be so hard to be patient. Don't rush through life. Stop and savor the moments you are living through. Be present and don't worry about or wish for the future. Every phase is important for your growth and the journey to adulthood.

When I was in high school, I couldn't wait to get out. I wasn't happy. I was scared and intimidated. Even though I was on student council and homecoming court, and had good grades and different groups of friends, my anxiety convinced me that I didn't fit in. I was so afraid of failing at something or failing someone that I just wanted the time to move fast so I could move away and go to college. My anxiety made me afraid of so many things that I wanted to move on and not face things. How silly, right? Going to college wasn't going to be any easier.

A little secret about me: I am an introvert and intuitive. What does that mean? It means I always felt weird and never felt secure in any environment. I was always analyzing and evaluating. Add anxiety to that, and it was hard for me to feel secure and trust friendships. I often preferred to spend time with my parents over friends. Bottom line: I just wanted to grow up fast, so I didn't have to deal with growing pains and peers.

Every minute, every hour, every day, every week of your life will be filled with choices and experiences—some good, some not so good. But, sitting in them is key to being able to learn, grow, and live a life worth living.

This may be hard to see now. Until you do the work to manage your anxious thoughts, you'll want to speed through every challenge, but try to live in each moment and learn from each experience.

WORRY

Worry:// mental distress or agitation resulting from concern usually for something impending or anticipated.

You can destroy your now by worrying about tomorrow.

JANIS JOPLIN

Worry is very similar to anxiety. In my opinion, worry is something we choose to allow whether we are anxious or not. For some people, anxiety has a genetic component and may be much more deeply seeded in the mind.

Some people are not happy unless they have something to worry about. They live focusing on the "what ifs" and not the "everything's okay unless I hear otherwise philosophy." These same people worry about things that are completely out of their control. They often assume the worst is going to happen instead of just letting life unfold.

Parents often fall into this trap. They worry about everything their child does from the moment they're born. Parents often become overprotective because they are afraid something terrible will happen to their child. What if their child goes to someone's house for a sleepover and something bad happens to them? What if they ride their bikes and get hit by a car? What if they don't get into the college they want to go to? Some parents struggle to quiet the "what if" thoughts.

You can see how worry is similar to anxiety, but anxiety may cause worry. Some people who worry a lot make the choice to worry. They simply choose to let their mind go in all what if directions. People with anxiety, however, aren't making a choice to worry. It happens innately, and they can't turn it off and change their thoughts as readily as someone who worries but doesn't have anxiety.

Here's an example: When my kids started driving, I let them drive to and from school. I could have worried about whether or not they made it there safely and been on pins and needles all day until they walked in the door that night. Instead, I said a prayer for their safety and sent them on their way, knowing that, if something were to happen, we'd deal with it at that time. I knew I couldn't control their actions while driving or the actions of other drivers. And I also knew that I couldn't sit in fear and worry all day, every day as I sent them off. If I hadn't made the choice to not worry, I would have driven myself crazy.

With anxiety, the emotions, fear, and what ifs are deeper than worry. I am not discounting worry, but we have a choice when it comes to worry. We may not have a choice as to whether or not we have anxiety.

Let's say you have a test coming up. You can worry and let your mind wonder over the "what if" thoughts: What if I fail? What if I get a bad grade? What if Sarah does better than me? What if I don't have time to study?

You have control over the time and effort you put into your test results and grades. You don't have control over the fact that you have anxiety, but you can control whether you take action to do the best possible. The difference in worrying and anxiety in this situation is that if you are worried, you may feel a little nervous, but you know you did the work and you can proceed to the test with some confidence. With anxiety, you may feel panicked, you may feel you can't take the test no matter how much you prepared, and you may experience a series of what ifs that you can't ignore and aren't realistic based your preparation. Feeling nervous is a pretty common emotion. Anxiety is more of an experience that can involve the whole body and mind. Many people may feel nervous, but seldom do the majority have anxious thoughts and feelings.

Worrying is less likely to prohibit you from taking action to earn the grades you desire. The same with playing sports or memorizing lines for a play. However, anxiety is more likely to hold you back completely. Anxiety can hold you back because of physical symptoms or because you simply can't quiet your mind. Some people experience complete shut down or mental blocks if anxiety is severe enough.

If you can differentiate between the two, you will find it easier to navigate. The more time and energy you put into worrying, the less time and energy you put into accomplishing your goals.

Both worry and anxiety take awareness to avoid or overcome. With worry, use the 5Cs strategy to catch the worry, challenge it, and change it.

Let's use a basketball game as an example. The game is Wednesday night at 7 p.m. You have practice to prepare on Monday and Tuesday. Before the first jump ball, you'll have plenty of time to warm up. On Monday morning, you start thinking about the Wednesday's game. You see yourself fouling out, missing every shot, or not being able to dribble. You've succumbed to the worry monster!

Stop and ask yourself: Has this ever happened in a game? Chances are the answer is no. Instead of working on your skills Monday and Tuesday, you worry about what might happened and aren't focused during practice. The result? You lose confidence, start making silly mistakes, and don't play up to your potential.

Had you not spent all that time worrying and instead spent time practicing with complete focus and positive energy, you could have visualized yourself doing well, and those worries would have not taken seed.

Thoughts of worry have the potential to influence the outcomes of everything you do. The most challenging part is that worry often accompanies anxiety. It's going to take more to overcome anxiety, but if you can work on the worry, which is more on the surface, you'll be able to make better, faster strides with navigating anxiety.

To help prevent overwhelm and decrease your mind's desire to worry, make lists. It not only feels great to cross accomplished items off of lists, but lists help keep you focused and help you stay on track. Having a list will help prevent missed assignments and serve as a reminder for what is required for you to do so you won't worry about missing something or forgetting to do something important. Small action items like making lists can save you from additional anxiety and worry. Your lists can be as long or short as you need them to be to help you keep the anxiety and worry at bay.

Another "to do" to help decrease worry is to set intentions. Each day set intentions about what your goals are and what action steps you'll take to achieve them. As you set your intentions, remember to give yourself the grace to adjust along the way because interruptions may occur. Be intentional about looking at the bumps in the road as opportunities to shift, and not to give up on the original intention to reach a goal or accomplish a task.

> Do not be anxious about anything, but in everything, by prayer and petition, with thanksgiving, present your requests to God. And the peace of God, which transcends

all understanding, will guard your hearts and minds in Christ Jesus.

PHILIPPIANS 4:6-7

PARENTS

By reading this chapter, you should have a pretty good idea of what anxiety looks like. One thing I want to emphasize is that anxiety can present at any age and in any way. For me, my anxiety manifested in physical symptoms at a very young age. The symptoms have remained consistent throughout my life.

My children have experienced a myriad of symptoms or indicators of underlying anxiety. None of them had the same two symptoms for the same amount of time, or at the same age as the other.

Other children experience totally different signs and symptoms than mine, but below is a list of things that you can think about as potential signs and symptoms, or indicators, that your child(ren) may have anxiety. This is not an all-inclusive list, but it is a list that friends, family, and I have observed.

- An inability to participate at birthday parties
- An inability to handle change
- OCD type of behaviors
- Headaches
- Stomachaches
- Irritability
- Anger
- Inability to sleep
- Dislike of crowds
- Dislike of loud noises
- Twirling the hair when nervous or stressed
- Pulling hair out, you may notice small patches of no hair
- An inability to eat or look at certain foods

- Skin sensitivities with clothing
- Mood swings

I am not saying that if your child has any of the above, they have anxiety. However, I want you to be aware that sometimes children will adapt certain reactions and behaviors because of underlying anxiety.

Think about it. We are all happiest and most settled when comfortable. This starts from infancy. When anxiety is present, it is harder to be comfortable, and when the unexpected is added into the mix, the challenge to be comfortable or at peace is even greater.

If you have noticed any of these signs and symptoms over the years along with any other indicators in this chapter, you may want to seek help and contact a therapist or mental health practitioner.

Here is another way to explain anxiety. Do you remember the game Red Rover? In elementary school, the teacher would choose two captains, and the captains would select members of their team. The teams then stood in lines about thirty feet apart. One team would then chant "red rover, red rover, send Nancy right over." Nancy from the other team would run and try to break through the linked arms of the chanting team. If she broke through, she got to take a person from the chanting team with her to her team. If she didn't break through the locked arms, she became a member of the chanting team.

Well, when everyone was standing in a large group for teams to be selected, I felt so much anxiety. Would I be picked first or would I be picked last? Most kids who are picked first are so happy to have been chosen. For me, it was a no-win situation. If I was selected first, yes, I was relieved to not be the last one standing, but I was also worried about whether someone else was upset that I was chosen before them, or what if I couldn't hold the link and disappointed the captain. So many what if thoughts. Whereas most kids just go with the flow and are excited to play, I was anxious the entire time.

It may seem silly, but this example demonstrates how the anxious mind can take away joy from a child, and how every day, completely normal situations can turn into an obstacle or challenge for a child with anxiety.

Anger

Anger:// a strong feeling of displeasure and usually of antagonism

 Where there is anger there is always pain underneath.

ECKHART TOLLE

ANXIETY CAN TRIGGER reactions of anger. Have you experienced anger to the point you think you are going to explode, and you have no idea why you are so angry, frustrated, agitated, or ready to scream at the next person that comes into sight?

I have. I used to let the irritability take over, and sometimes anger quickly followed. I would become irritated at my family and be disrespectful to them or yell at them. I was agitated because of anxiety, not able to handle unknowns or lack of control over a situation. The agitation made me overreact to situations or people.

It may have been that we were running late. Maybe we were traveling, and I couldn't handle the anxiety of the unknown. It might have been the fear of making the wrong decision and having to face disappointment or disappointing others. It may have been that I had to attend a party and the anxiety of not knowing what to wear or who would be in attendance would strike a match in my body that lit a flame of irritation and annoyance.

My father had the same reaction. He was often accused of having a bad temper. This may have been true but knowing now what I know about anxiety, I believe he suffered from anxiety and had no idea how to deal with it. When he was young, it was taboo to talk about mental health issues. Society associated mental health challenges such as anxiety or depression as weaknesses. Mental health was a forbidden topic of conversation, a skeleton hidden in a closet of secrecy. How was he to get help if it burdened him with social stereotypes and judgment?

It wasn't until I learned more about anxiety that I realized what was happening. I cannot take credit for this wisdom. I spent months in therapy to help me navigate the emotions of anxiety. Finally, I learned to hesitate, and evaluate my thoughts and the situation, before reacting. I have to take the time to identify the emotions I am feeling and then evaluate what is causing the feelings. Situational anxiety is almost always the root cause.

If I catch the thoughts, challenge them, and then change them, following the 5Cs journaling method, I can stave off a negative reaction and prevent hurt feelings. Does it work every time? No, sometimes the anxiety wins, but having a strategy to follow when my emotions feel threatening helps me minimize or prevent the negative reactions.

It's important to note that anger is not a bad emotion. Anger is an emotion we have every right to feel and express. The goal is to express it without causing hurt feelings for someone else or injuring ourselves.

No one should ever accept being mistreated, bullied, or abused. Sometimes even immense disappointment can cause us to be angry. When such events occur, anger is stimulated and may be an appropriate reaction. How we channel the anger determines its value to our lives and emotional status. Temporary anger is healthy and protective, holding on to anger can be destructive. When feeling angry, it is best to assess the source and evaluate the severity of responsive actions. Anger, when not appropriately channeled, can cause hurt and more anger. Relationships can be damaged when anger is permitted to take control.

We have no control over how other people behave or treat us. With that said, people may treat us in ways that we don't appreciate, that trigger our anxiety, and result in anger being the end emotion, hopefully temporarily.

What happens when we feel questioned or attacked, or when someone isn't being kind to us? Anxious thoughts arise quickly and prevent us from rationalizing the situation. It's kind of like the flight or fight mechanism. Our anxiety immediately makes us feel attacked, and we either flee or we fight.

Interestingly, our brain quickly identifies and holds onto negative thoughts and experiences. This fact makes it hard to forget or keep our reactions to threatening situations in check.

Here's an example. It's kind of ugly, certainly not a pretty memory for me from when I was about sixteen. My mom, whom I love, grew up in a very dysfunctional family. She was also a teen mom, having me at seventeen. That meant, she was still extremely young when I was growing up and we sort of grew up together. When I say she always tried to do what was best for my sisters and me, I am not exaggerating. We are all good humans with great lives as adult women who care deeply for others and have hearts of service. But, growing up things weren't always roses and butterflies.

Because of her life experiences she had trouble trusting other people. One time she accused me of something, and I hadn't done it. I don't recall what that something was, but I knew I was innocent. And, for the record, I was a terrible liar. When I tried to sneak or do things behind my parents' backs, I always got caught (one of the disadvantages of living in a small town in the middle of nowhere).

To give perspective, the dining room was right off the kitchen. She was standing at the kitchen counter, which was in a U-shape, and I was sitting at the dining room table, where I was told to sit. As she asked me the same question a million different ways to get me to change my answer and prove she was right, my anxiety grew. I felt trapped. I couldn't flee the situation because then I would have been spanked or grounded. The more anxious and frustrated I became, the angrier I became. I felt hopeless and attacked.

This is one of those moments I wish I could forget, but it stuck with me as some significant, yet bad memories do. I pushed a lot of memories and experiences from my teens and twenties out of my mind. I intentionally chose not to remember them because I was either ashamed of them, or they hurt too much to revisit them. Part of me wishes I could remember them now so that I could give you more examples of how anxiety affected me, but I repressed them because I needed to navigate life as positively as possible.

Anyway, back to the story. My anger continued to build as my mom kept at me. It was a screaming match, and when anything gets to that point, it's best to walk away, but that wasn't an option for me. Then, out of sheer frustration, overwhelm, and hot anger, my mind started spinning and my breath came in shorter and shorter waves, and I banged my head on the table—so hard that I bent the ring on my hand with the impact.

To say I snapped is an understatement. I was so angry that this was my life and now I was physically hurting on top of the emotional turmoil I was feeling, and I was still in trouble for something I did not do.

This incident was the beginning of a pattern of self-injurious behavior. When I was studying for exams, the anxiety would filter in and distract me. Constant distractions of my mind being on a Ferris wheel of negative thoughts convincing me that I couldn't focus, I couldn't learn, and reminding me of the what ifs of failure. I would get so frustrated. The Ferris wheel feels like an apt analogy for how anxiety feels. Negative thoughts board the wheel, the Ferris Wheel (our minds) spins faster and faster, not stopping to allow positive thoughts to board or negative thoughts to disembark.

During those times I may have acted rude, I might have recoiled into myself, or I might have inflicted pain on myself until I brought myself out of it and was able to refocus. These incidents didn't happen often, but it happened any time my brain got stuck in a pattern of negative thoughts. I didn't know then that it was anxiety. I thought I was crazy. I thought I was stupid. I thought I was worthless. Those thoughts made me hate myself and resulted in more anger. Looking back, I must have seemed completely out of my mind to the angels in the room (I never did any of these things in front of another human).

Several years ago, I taught a photography camp for teens. One of the girls in the camp struggled with severe anxiety. It was a big accomplishment that she was able to attend the camp. Each day, I took the kids out on the college campus, and we explored and practiced the photography skills I taught that morning. The next morning, I shared their images, and we got to see the really cool things each other captured, and I was able to give advice if the students wanted it.

One of the images was of a snail on this girl's arm. One of the boys, innocently with no malice intended, said, "Who's arm is that that's so hairy?"

I knew who the arm belonged to and knew to look for her reaction. She got up and left the classroom. The assistant in the classroom took over, and I went out to see if the girl was okay. She was not. She was so angry that she wanted to hurt someone. She said over and over how much she hated herself and how much she wanted to hurt the boy. Unfortunately, I was not able to calm her down, and the camp nurse had to come to take care of her. Her mother came shortly thereafter and took her home. She never came back to camp.

I tell this story because it is a very real example of a teen girl being hurt, having held onto negative thoughts from others for years, and being unable to filter the comment as harmless from a silly, immature boy versus a malicious, statement meant to hurt her. Anxiety causes the brain to get off track, or to stay on the track that is negative instead of transferring tracks at the positive station.

Anxiety causes a misconception that we should be perfect. Because if things aren't perfect, something bad will happen. I remember panicking over an outfit not looking right, my hair not doing what I wanted, running late, studying, or when a friend backing out and having to go someplace alone instead of having the security of someone I trusted by my side.

Any of these situations could have sent me into a tailspin because my mind was set on one thing, one way, one vision, and when that did not workout, the anxiety mounted, suffocating me, and the only way I could breathe again was to hurt myself to bring myself back to the moment.

I feel so vulnerable writing this. It brings tears to my eyes to think of how dysfunctional I was. And that brings me to the next emotion in the equation: shame. Anger drives shame. Shame goads anger. Shame triggers anxiety. Learning to recognize our feelings, symptoms, and responses to each, is not an option; it is a necessity, or we will live in a vicious cycle of anxiety, anger, shame, and anxiety. I can't stress enough the importance of identifying the triggers of anxiety that lead to anger. Be able to recognize them so that the second they arise, you can take control of your thoughts and actions. Doing so will help alleviate regret and shame. We'll talk more about shame in the next chapter.

In the example above where I banged my head on the table, I felt such shame. To this day, my heart skips a beat and my stomach surges to think about it. I felt shame because I couldn't control myself. I felt shame because I felt so much hate. I also had to live with the embarrassment of a goose egg on my forehead for a week, which was a constant reminder of the shame I felt.

What is important to note is that anger will result in us needing to ask for forgiveness, having to forgive others, and forgiving ourselves. It was not easy for me to forgive myself or the times I became angry because shame was beating me up. Looking back, I was in the throes of deep anxiety that I did not understand or recognize, and I had to give myself grace eventually and move on.

Here's another example. One time, I was going to break up with a boyfriend. He was a handsome, sweet guy, and I really liked him, but we weren't aligned in our goals and dreams for the future. Instead of simply telling him I did not want to date him anymore, I freaked out. My anxiety caused me to be so irrational. I became angry at him for no reason. I'm certain he thought I was nuts. There was absolutely no excuse for my behavior other than my anxiety triggered the fear, which triggered anger, and I wasn't kind. I blamed him for me wanting to break up with him, and he had not done anything wrong. I was so anxious that I couldn't come up with the right things to say, and instead blamed him instead of taking ownership as I should have. It can be very humbling to have to apologize. The sooner we can get a grasp on anxiety, the less anger, the less shame, and the fewer times we need to humble ourselves to apologize and ask for forgiveness.

FORGIVENESS

What is forgiveness? Forgiveness, according to psychologists, is the intentional releasing of feelings of resentment or anger toward someone, or a group of people, who have hurt you, whether you believe they deserve it or not. Forgiving does not mean that you are forgetting, ignoring, or denying the seriousness of the offense against you.

When we forgive, we no longer harbor deep anger towards someone and find peace of mind. I can't answer the question of whether true forgiveness results in positive feelings toward a person who hurt you, but at the very least it does reduce the negative feelings you'll carry around about the person. Think of it as being able to let go of the pain you felt and empowering yourself to heal from the hurtful situation. Forgiveness is something that is still being studied by scientists in the mental health field.

I think of forgiveness as a gift. It is always important to forgive others. We may not forget what they've done or said, but we get to forgive and choose to live a peaceful life. It is also important to forgive ourselves. We can't live a meaningful life if we are angry at ourselves or others. Yes, we will do things wrong, we will say hurtful things, we will let anger take control of our actions. However, we cannot live in those moments forever. How miserable that would be. Forgive yourself, ask others for forgiveness, receive the forgiveness they offer, and forgive them in return. It's humbling, for sure, but if we take the road of humility, we will be able to build and maintain healthy relationships with others and, equally as important, ourselves.

Forgiveness will help alleviate anger and shame. Let me share a story of forgiveness with you. When I was in college, I had an abusive boyfriend. He was domineering, controlling, demanding, hurtful, manipulative, and mean. I finally woke up and realized what was happening. I had missed out on a lot of great fun and memories with my friends because I wasn't "allowed" to go out without him or a fight would ensue, sometimes emotional, sometimes physical. He was jealous. Looking back, I am sure his jealousy was a response to his own cheating and inability to be honest and faithful.

When he cheated on me for the third (to my knowledge) time, I had finally had enough. To say he hurt me is an understatement. My anxiety, though, also kept me planted in the relationship. I was so insecure and had such a lack of self-esteem and trust in myself that I was afraid if I didn't have him, I'd have no one. He had helped to convince me of that as well.

For years I felt shame. In fact, it wasn't until recently that I approached the subject with my best girlfriends from college and admitted what had happened during those years. The shame I felt was related to letting him treat me like that, for not sticking up for myself, for letting down my friends, and secluding myself instead of being in the prime of life with them. I was embarrassed and ashamed.

When I finally woke up and realized I had to get out of the relationship, I could have chosen to let hate and anger fester in my heart for the rest of my life, but I decided very early on to forgive. I'll never forget, but I have peace and almost feel sorry for him because it can't be pleasant to live with that much hate and control in your heart.

I also had to forgive myself. I had to forgive myself for letting it happen so I could release the shame. He may not care whether I forgave him, but not having that anger and hurt inside my heart gave me peace of mind and the grace to move forward with other relationships. It took me a long time to truly trust in relationships. Once betrayed, it's hard to be vulnerable and open, and to love and trust again, but it is possible.

PARENTS

 Children emulate adult behaviors.

Anger. It's an unavoidable emotion, but some of us handle it better than others. As indicated in this chapter, I've had plenty of experience with anger and anxiety.

I loved my father dearly, but his temper was terrible. He knew it, and he tried to control it. But, when you don't know the source of the problem, how can you fix it? I believe with all my heart that he suffered from anxiety, and when situations occurred that were not what he had expected or what he had planned for, instead of going with the flow and moving through the experience, he became angry. This has happened to me too. It isn't pleasant, and it is a hard reaction to explain.

Here is my attempt: We push through all the time, and then we reach a limit. Everyone has experienced the sleeping bear effect. The bear will sleep through just about everything, but when nudged one too many times, you better run!

The same happens with anxiety. There are certain things that the brain can handle and adapt to, but when anxiety takes control, the result is a reaction like bears being nudged too many times.

It's like there is a switch. Everything's fine, and then suddenly, the switch is flipped and instead of adapting, anxiety triggers the fight mechanism in the amygdala part of the brain. All bets may be off, or you may be able to point out that "it's okay" and calm your child(ren) down. Chances are, you will be the one she is lashing out at, and she may not be in a state of mind to listen to you.

Maybe she is running late. It isn't your fault that she is running late, but you are driving her to whatever she is late for, and she gets snippy with you, is rude to you, and blames you. Blame often accompanies anger because people don't like to admit faults. It's so much easier to blame someone else. And it's quite possible that they don't understand the reaction occurring. They don't want to react negatively, but their brain is experiencing a hiccup.

It's like I've said to my children: I'll be your "punching bag" for as long as you need me to so that you can be kind to everyone else, but if you cross a line, you will be grounded. Because I've suffered from anxiety, I knew what's happening. They are in a state of panic. Their brain is in "fight" mode, trying to keep themselves above water.

As parents, we have a choice. We can get angry right back at them, or we can remind ourselves what's happening. If we stay calm, they will most likely settle into the moment too. If we, however, react with scolding them, yelling at them, or grounding them, the situation may become a screaming match.

I am in no way justifying disrespectful behavior, but when children have anxiety, they often don't realize what is happening, or how rude and nasty they sound. This is where we come in to help them recognize and manage these reactions and get them the help they need through therapy.

Remember, they've been doing their best to keep themselves in check with everyone else all day, every day. It is exhausting, and sometimes they simply can't hold it in any longer. They trust you to always love them and support them, so they unleash in front of you. Most often, there is no maliciousness toward you; it's a matter of feeling safe to be who and what they need to be in the moment.

As I type this, it sounds a bit irrational, but the mind is so complicated, and it can be hard to navigate whether these behaviors are triggered by anxiety or simply "normal" teen behaviors.

Compare the prevalence of angry reactions to the presence of other symptoms mentioned before. If there are more signs and symptoms than anger, it might be an indication that it is time for an evaluation with a professional, your pediatrician, or a therapist.

It might not be you that your child(ren) reacts to. It may be their siblings. A sibling can do the slightest thing and a child with anxiety may completely overreact. What I learned over the years is that when one child has something like anxiety that the other doesn't, they don't understand each other. A child with no anxiety will not be able to relate to or understand why a child with anxiety is acting, reacting, or responding the way they are. Likewise, if another child has a learning challenge, the child with anxiety may not understand the need for complete quiet or the need for special resources for the child with learning challenges. And, if a child is empathetic, she may take on the "suffering" of the other child, wanting to help but not being able to. This causes a realm of challenges in and of itself.

I think the key takeaway here, and something I have had to work hard on, is to keep my own emotions in check and focus on helping my child. I am very excitable and when I get excited, I tend to raise my voice, not out of anger, more out of excitement and passion. Unfortunately, my excited reaction has often been interpreted as yelling. Then, my child would react with more negative behavior toward me. The more I stay calm, the better the situations are because we can navigate them together.

Patience has also been key. I have not been a patient person, but I have had to become more patient to help my children navigate the world. One thing I've learned is that impatience never brings success, but patience does. The more patient we can be, the more helpful we will be for our children.

There is no overnight fix for anxiety. It's important to work on patience and embrace the journey to overcome anxiety because it may take months to see progress, and the anxiety may never go away. The key will be to implement a management and treatment strategy so that the anxiety doesn't worsen, and hopefully improves.

On the flip side, some children may appear angry, but they are withdrawing. This is when they are more quiet than usual, or not interested in speaking to you. Try not to get angry with them but give them space to navigate their emotions and feelings. Let them know that when they are ready, you will be there for them, but until then, you will give them their space. Doing so will allow your child to work through her emotions and come to a solution on her own. It may be hard for you not to spend the time worrying while she is working through her emotions, but as long as you know she is safe, you can go about your activities, and check in in a couple of hours or wait patiently until she is ready to come to you.

Lastly, before we close out the chapter on anger, I want to mention one more thing. Sometimes, when kids have a learning challenge that hasn't been diagnosed, they may display more anger than usual. Case in point, we've been blessed with very bright children. One of my boys never did homework, and we were always baffled with how good his standardized test scores and grades were. The only thing he ever struggled with was writing. I asked for help from his teachers and was told he needed to practice picking up pennies to help with fine motor skills. The more I observed him and the ideas he had and how well he could articulate verbally, I knew there was something more than fine motor skills.

Because the school wouldn't help us, I went to a private occupational therapist. She discovered that my son had sensory integration disorder. She worked with him for months, and he improved. He did above average all the way through elementary and middle school. But, when he got to high school, the information was coming in faster and was much harder, and he began to fall behind.

At first, we pushed him to do more work. Then we started to see shifts in behavior. He was moody and angry—not his jovial, happy-go-lucky self. One night everything came to a head, and I was at a complete loss (my husband was traveling for work). The next morning, I called the guidance counselor at his school. After going through everything, he suggested we have my son tested for a learning disability.

My gut had been right. After going through the extensive testing process, he was diagnosed with severe processing and retrieval challenges and ADHD. Another God wink for us. We had chosen to send the boys to Catholic school for a smaller learning environment. We were able to get him the help he needed to navigate his new diagnosis, and he went back to doing extremely well in school.

This story may not appear to have anything to do with anxiety, but it does. The more he struggled, the more anxious he became about school and the work ahead of him. The more anxious he became, the less he could focus and the more stupid he felt. After a sixth grade teacher had called him stupid, he began to use that term for himself when he wasn't feeling accomplished in school. We knew this wasn't true. I never had a doubt in mind that he was incredibly bright, and his IQ tests proved it. After receiving the help he needed, he was able to recognize that he wasn't stupid and finally believed me!

I share this story because it is possible that if your child is experiencing anxiety related to school, or significant behavioral changes, there may be an underlying issue. As you deal with the anxiety, I suggest not leaving any stones unturned. Most importantly, follow your parental instincts.

Shame

Shame:// a condition of humiliating disgrace or disrepute; a painful emotion caused by consciousness of guilt, shortcoming, or impropriety

 The difference between shame and guilt is the difference between "I am bad" and "I did something bad."

BRENÉ BROWN

PEOPLE WITH ANXIETY realize there is something different about them. We lack confidence and often self-esteem. We observe how others can walk into a room and talk to everyone else with ease. It looks like they show up not worried about a thing. They laugh and just be themselves when we have to double, triple, even quadruple analyze things.

We also realize that relationships are harder to build and maintain because we lack trust in ourselves and for others. We constantly wonder and worry about what others are thinking about us, and whether we did and said the right thing.

We struggle with living in the moment and question everything. We don't like surprises because we want to be in control of every situation to make sure nothing bad will happen.

These struggles result in blame. People with anxiety blame themselves for not being able to build and maintain relationships. We blame ourselves for being weird, or for disappointing ourselves and others. This blame results in shame.

When we experience shame because of anxiety, the definition is altered. Shame is usually a painful feeling of humiliation or distress caused by the consciousness of wrong or foolish behavior. In the case of anxiety, however, it is an interpretation of said behavior, not an actual act of doing something wrong or being foolish.

Approximately thirty to fifty percent of generalized anxiety disorder is related to genetics. It's important to note that there are multiple types of anxiety from generalized anxiety disorder to panic disorder, social anxiety, and even phobias. Each type may have different generic statistics, but the one thing in common is this: If you have blood relatives with anxiety or mental illness, you are at a higher risk of having anxiety.

When you start to beat yourself up over the fact that you have anxiety, remember you didn't choose your DNA or the experiences in life that may have triggered your anxiety. For this reason, you cannot blame yourself for your anxiety. While it is best to not allow yourself to feel shame because of anxiety, it will likely occur, and it will take work to eliminate it. Instead of using valuable energy feeling shame, take that energy and try to apply it to learning mechanisms for navigating the anxiety.

Instead of being embarrassed about your anxiety, own it. I promise you that your peers have similar or different struggles, and you are not alone. If you own your anxiety, now that you know what it is, you may even be able to help others with their anxiety, after you've begun managing your own safely and effectively, of course.

It only takes one word for someone to make you feel better. It only takes one smile to make someone else feel valuable. If others know you have anxiety, if you know others have anxiety, you can form a community to hold each other up and support each other. If you aren't sure how to form a community or club for teens with anxiety, ask your guidance counselor at school or your paster at church. Or maybe one of your parents or your therapist can help you organize it.

Find others who are going through similar challenges as you and build a support system of peers. Taking action is always better than being still and trying to hide because we are afraid of what others might think about us. One small action may make a huge impact on someone else and their quality of life as well as your own.

There is no such thing as normal. Each human on this earth was created by God to be unique, to be special, to be individuals. You are you, and instead of punishing yourself by feeling shame or blame, realize you are beautifully created to live a life of love, joy, service, and hope.

God will take the blame and shame from you. Pray daily asking God to take the blame and shame from your heart and give you peace to smile and embrace yourself as the wonderful human He made you to be, whom you are.

Pray: Dear Lord, please quiet my mind and calm my heart so that I may live the life you have planned for me. In Jesus name, Amen.

When you have a moment of shame, stop and write down something good about yourself. That may seem impossible today, but I promise you that if you try, you will be able to find something amazing about yourself every single day. It doesn't matter if the only thing you can think of right now is that you were able to get out of bed and take a shower. That is a start.

If you really think about it, I bet there is a list to fill an entire notebook page of wonderful things about you. Your eyes are beautiful and have a sparkle when you smile. You were nice to someone in the hallway yesterday. You got a good grade on a test. You exercised last night. You made someone smile today. I am absolutely positive there is something you are amazing at. Embrace it and focus on the good, not the bad. Journaling will help you begin to recognize the good and diminish the shame.

I am not making light of the feelings you feel every day. I know they are real. I know because I have probably experienced most of them myself. What I want to do is share with you the steps that have helped me move out of a place of constant anxiety and darkness to a place of light and hope.

Fear instigates shame, and in return, shame instigates fear. If we succumb to one, we succumb to both, and life becomes dark and lonely.

Talking and communicating is an important step to overcoming shame. In her book *The Gifts of Imperfection*, Brené Brown writes, "The less we talk about shame, the more control it has over our lives." Brené defines shame as the intensely painful feeling or experience of believing that we are flawed and therefore unworthy of love and belonging.

If you don't have someone to talk about your feelings of shame with, do the following exercise. List your feelings of shame, and then think of something positive and a reason to let go of that shame. As you go through this exercise, remember that shame is based on the fear that you are unlovable for whatever reason you've convinced yourself of.

The Feeling of Shame that is Consuming Me	Why I am Worthy and Can Release this Feeling of Shame
I was rude to my mom	I apologized and mom forgave me
I failed my geometry test, everyone else has a better grade	I worked hard, I talked to my teacher, I have As in all of my other subjects
I didn't make the basketball team	I did my best, I can work hard and try again next year if I still want to make the team, I tried out even though I was afraid

Shame is an emotion that a lot of people experience, not just you or those with anxiety. It's a common emotion that embeds in our brains because we've been convinced we aren't worthy. Anxiety is a major culprit in convincing us we aren't worthy.

Doing the exercise above will help you realize where your shame is coming from and help you overcome the feelings of unworthiness.

∼

PARENTS

In the last chapter I addressed anger. Anger leads to shame. If your child has been rude to you, disrespectful, or done anything they are ashamed of, they may need space to overcome the shame.

There are a few things to note related to shame. Just like you shouldn't blame yourself for your child's anxiety, it is important not to feel shame for their diagnosis.

Like I mentioned at the very beginning of the book, anxiety frequently has a genetic component, and genetics are not something we can control. Likewise, we cannot control what happens in a child's brain or how they respond to different stimuli. Mental health has been stereotyped over the years because there was a lack of information available. Anxiety, depression, and learning disabilities are not things to be ashamed of. We aren't ashamed if our children have a diagnosis of diabetes, heart problems, or cancer. So, why do we feel the need to be ashamed of a diagnosis of anxiety or anything related to the brain?

When my son's anxiety was at its height of severity, we had to accept that we had to let him quit lacrosse to navigate the anxiety and OCD resulting from the anxiety. Lacrosse was our life. He wanted to play in college, and many of our friends were in the lacrosse circle. We felt such a great sense of loss and because he was struggling with anxiety, we felt like we couldn't tell anyone what was going on. I was never ashamed, but I felt so protective of him. I didn't want other kids to make fun of him or think he was crazy because he was experiencing this hiccup with his brain. His coach knew and guided us to the best possible therapist, thank God. As we left the carpool and people asked why we weren't at lacrosse, we simply said he was having some medical challenges. That is part of the reason I am writing this book. We shouldn't have to worry about shaming or being embarrassed by mental health challenges.

The prevalence of anxiety is at an all-time high, and I don't see it abating. It's time to make anxiety and depression topics of conversation that people aren't afraid of.

Many people have questions about anxiety, but they are afraid to ask. When I have mentioned that my child has anxiety, people respond with a sense of relief. They are grateful they aren't alone. Chances are, there are others in your circle of friends who have a child or children with anxiety too.

Shame isn't only about the diagnosis. In the story of my son with the learning challenges, I felt guilt and shame that I hadn't pushed harder and had let the public school district push his challenges aside all those years ago. I felt shame and guilt that I hadn't done more to pursue help for him at that time. When I expressed that to the neuropsychiatrist, he said to me, "Robyn, this is not your fault. Your son is incredibly bright, and with his test scores and grades, I wouldn't have tested my child either. Processing and retrieval challenges most often do not present until the information they are learning is harder and coming in at a faster pace." I cried with relief.

I share this with you because as a parent, we so often sit with quilt and shame. It can become unbearable, but if we let those feelings take over, we will not be able to care for ourselves so that we can care for our child(ren).

Likewise, if you are feeling shame about your reactions to your child, give yourself grace. We all make mistakes. In the next chapter, I address fear and how fear can trigger anger and yelling.

I used to beat myself up at the end of the day because I wasn't the perfect mother and every other mom I knew seemed like the perfect mom. But there is no such thing as perfect, and I was bound to make mistakes. I eventually learned that my friends were not perfect parents either.

The most important thing you can do is work on your own mindfulness about your past and the experiences you have had, and realize we often mirror what we have experienced and learned. But you can change. You can break negative patterns and be the parent you want to be.

If you are feeling shame about how you parented in the past, one of the most therapeutic things you can do is to apologize to your child. Communicate with them and give them an understanding of why you reacted the way you did. Create a plan for times when such reactions have happened in the past so you can move forward with positive steps.

Fear

Fear:// an unpleasant often strong emotion caused by anticipation or awareness of danger.

 The only thing to fear is fear itself.

FRANKLIN DELANO ROOSEVELT

DID you know that social anxiety is a fear? It is the fear of judgement, evaluation, or rejection by others. Social anxiety may also be referred to as social phobia, and it is the main reason people struggle with public speaking.

Fear is a basic emotion that we are born with. When we sense danger, our nervous system is stimulated and reacts quickly.

Fear is our brain's reaction to protect us and to help us survive. When we experience fear, our nervous system kicks in, and we experience a reaction of fight, flight, or being frozen, unable to move or react. Our brain will stay in this state until the threat, or assumed threat, disappears, and our brain recognizes everything is safe.

Fear kept our ancestors alive and still does the same for us. It's an emotional reaction to a situation, circumstance, or person that our brain sees as a trigger or threat to our physical, emotional or psychological well-being. Fear helps us reduce or remove harm from our lives. It protects us.

 Fear is one of the seven universal emotions experienced by everyone around the world. Fear arises with the threat of harm, either physical, emotional, or psychological, real or imagined. While traditionally considered a "negative" emotion, fear actually serves an important role in keeping us safe as it mobilizes us to cope with potential danger.

PAUL EKMAN

I both love and hate President Franklin D. Roosevelt's quote shared at the beginning of this chapter. Had you heard that quote before? Fear is a reality that those of us with anxiety live with every day. "Stop being afraid," they say. "Stop being afraid to try," they say. "Stop worrying about it and just do it," they say.

They say a lot of things, but to those of us who are experiencing fear related to anxiety, we are not able to turn the fear off. In fact, quite often, the more people say "stop" to us, the more afraid we become.

Our brains are created with the flight or fight mechanism to keep us safe. When we have anxiety, our brain experiences hiccups that prevents us from changing our thoughts from fear or flight, to going for it, thinking it's easy, or that it will be okay. Instead, our brains are on a Ferris Wheel two hundred feet up in the air, and the fearful thoughts keep getting on the ride, but none of these thoughts are getting off. This cycle continues until our brain can recognize that it is not being rational, the ride must stop, and the negative, fearful thoughts must get off.

Anxiety is often driven by fear, such as fear of making mistakes, fear of failure, fear of embarrassment, and fear of not being accepted. Those fears can also cause anxiety.

Let me share a couple of stories about fear. The elementary school I attended went from kindergarten to eighth grade. It was there that I discovered a love for basketball. From fifth grade to eighth grade, my father coached my team, and I practiced every day. I loved it and wanted to be the best. I made the all-conference team my eighth-grade year when playing against some pretty amazing girls. You would think that I would have been able to try out for the high school team and feel confident that I could make it, at least the junior varsity team.

But I didn't. My anxiety took hold of my reasoning and fear set in, big time. Or maybe it was the other way around and fear took hold and anxiety set in.

I didn't even try out for the team. I made all kinds of excuses; I wish I could remember them all. Studying, chores, you name it. Anything so I wouldn't have to try out and risk not making the team.

To this day, I look back on that decision and wish I made a different decision. But, I also know that everything happens for a reason, and my life turned out just fine.

In a previous chapter, I shared a story from several years later, when I was working on my doctorate degree in pharmacy. My fear of public speaking interfered with my goals and dreams. I temporarily quit but still had a happy ending. It's probably because my mom, daddy, and grandma were always praying for me. I was "blessed!"

And anxiety didn't just stop me from going for big goals. Anxiety also kept me from doing things I wanted to do, like raising a hand in class, sleeping over at friends' houses, or going on spring break trips.

Many times, when people quit or don't do things because of fear, they miss out on amazing opportunities, chances to make memories, discover the world, or build relationships. Before quitting, stop and evaluate the root of your fear. Dive deeply into your heart and mind. Pray about your fear. Talk to people about your fear. Don't quit because you think that is the only answer. Talking about your emotions can help you find a way past the fear and to the path of fun, joy, and success.

Now, if you ask me to get on a stage and speak to a group, I will gladly do it. Am I afraid, heck yes! Through prayer and the ability to reason with myself, I am able to talk myself out of debilitating fear, get my mind to stop the Ferris Wheel, kick negative thoughts off, and let positive thoughts on. That is a tremendous accomplishment in and of itself! I hope you will be able to experience it, too.

A lot of my anxiety and fear have been related to failure. I've since learned that failure is not something to be afraid of. Embrace that thought now, while you are young. If you fail, you are opening the door to success later. Every failure is a learning opportunity that will make you better, stronger, and wiser. When you are feeling afraid and know it is part of your anxiety, or vice versa, stop for a moment, and catch those thoughts in action. Then challenge those thoughts. Ask yourself if the thoughts are warranted. Most likely the thoughts are because you are trying something new or putting yourself out in the world in a way that is terrifying, but you can change those thoughts to be positive enough to get you through the anxiety, over the fear, and on to bigger and amazing experiences.

When experiencing fear, realize that life is full of deep, shadowed valleys. The question is can you find a way to climb out of the valley back up to the light at the peak, which is waiting for you. The answer: YES, you can! We all can. Maybe not alone, but together, we can. The key to reaching the light is putting one foot in front of the other, journaling one thought after the other, going to therapy, meditating, and/or tapping into your faith and praying. The right action is specific to you and what works for you, everyone is unique in their response to various solutions, but taking action is the only way to overcome fear and anxiety.

I know you are going to feel alone sometimes. I've felt that way too, many, many times. If you allow yourself to put fear aside, be vulnerable, and ask for help, you will no longer be alone. You are loved, and no matter how frightening life seems, there will always be someone in your corner to lift you up, to help you find answers, and to stand by you. It may take time to trust someone, but if you are willing to try, you will find the person that will become your "go to," your rock, your steady, your strength and support. The person you can go to when you feel afraid or alone. If you aren't ready to trust a person with your anxieties and fears, you can always turn to your faith.

Remember Roosevelt's quote about having nothing to fear but fear itself? This phrase infers that fear will hold us back and prevent us from finding joy. Fear could prevent us from living the life we've been given. Sure, there will be things in life that we fear, but we don't have to sit and worry about things happening that we need to be afraid of.

The more time we spend with negative, fearful thoughts, the more likely something bad will happen. Instead of worrying and being fearful, transform those thoughts to gratitude and positive what ifs. If you are thinking what if I get in a car accident and get hurt and can't go to school, change that thought to, "I will drive safely, be cautious, and get to the appointment on time."

Note how you felt when you said what if I get in a car accident and get hurt and can't go to school? You probably felt anxious, sad, fearful—maybe you had a physical reaction to the thoughts. Those negative thoughts turned into negative feelings. When that happens, we don't take action and we have zero results.

Now how did you feel when you said I will drive safely, be cautious, and get the appointment on time and safely? Did you feel relieved, happy, secure, confident? Most likely, yes. When you approach having to drive with positive thoughts and feelings, you will be able to get in the car, and drive yourself to the appointment, and get the results you need.

The bright side is that while a negative mindset will leave you discouraged and miserable, a positive mindset brings positive things. We'll learn more about using the 5Cs journaling method to channel a positive mindset in the chapter entitled, "The 5Cs Journaling Method."

Meanwhile, before we move through the next several chapters, I want you to embrace fears you've had, but leave them here, right here on this page, and move through each topic with an open mind. Remember that your goal is to learn and grow to overcome the fear that has previously held you back.

Fearful Thought	Feelings created by the fearful thought	New positive thought	Feelings created by the new positive thought
No one likes me	Sad, lonely, afraid	Sara is my friend, and she is nice to me	Happy, content, excited
I am going to fail this geometry test	Sad, scared, overwhelmed, frustrated	I have been studying so much, and I met with my tutor, I will do my best	Relieved, nervous but confident
What if the plane crashes	Scared, overwhelmed, confused, conflicted, sad	I can't wait to see Grandma, plane crashes don't happen very often, my parents will be with me	Relieved, excited, happy

COURAGE

Now, let's switch gears a little and talk about courage. Courage is when you have the mental or moral strength to venture, persevere, and withstand danger, fear, or difficulty

Courage is not the opposite of fear. It is the ability to take action despite the fact that fear is present. Fear will hold you back. It will tell you to stay put and stay safe. The problem with listening to fear is that you won't grow, change, overcome anxiety, or live a joyful life.

Courage comes from deep within you. It lives at the core of your being. It's like curiosity; you were born with it and it's just waiting for you to call it forth.

Taking one step at a time, saying yes to one invite at a time, saying one positive word to yourself every day, is courage.

The more you tap into your inner courage, the more you'll be able to quiet your anxiety.

I'm not going to tell you that being courageous is easy. It's not, and it takes practice. But, if you never begin to tap into your courageous spirit, you'll never be able to grow and do the things you are dreaming of.

Go ahead, do one small courageous thing today and then another tomorrow and another the day after that...and just keep going.

Remember the Cowardly Lion in *The Wizard of Oz*? He was on a quest for courage. When he met Scarecrow, Tin Man, and Dorothy, they told him the Wizard may be able to help him by giving him courage. The wizard gave him something to drink for courage, but what the wizard said was much more meaningful than the regular old liquid with no magical properties.

The wizard told the lion that he was a victim of disorganized thoughts. Little did the wizard know that he was describing anxiety and how it causes fear. Anxiety is an array of disorganized thoughts. Thoughts dancing in our heads, making a lot of noise without true meaning or purpose. They are mostly negative "what ifs."

The anxious thoughts are often not rational, and they get stuck, like a hamster on a wheel. The thoughts spin and spin until they've created a web of lies: I can't do this, I am not good enough, I'm a failure, something bad will happen, I'm fat, I'm ugly, they won't like me, on and on.

Courage gives us the opportunity to recognize the negative, anxious thought patterns. It takes courage to catch the thoughts, challenge them, and change them. That courage is within you, in your heart and soul. If you believe that, and tap into it as a resource, you can move past fear and into life experiences with more ease and less overwhelm.

Tapping into your courage will take practice and work. It may not happen overnight. It's a thought shift, and anytime we are working on a thought shift, we have to give ourselves grace and patience. The mind is tricky and quickly reverts back into the old thought patterns of anxiety and fear. Use your courage to push those thoughts out of the way so you can make your way forward.

How is bravery different than courage? Bravery is tapping into courage to demonstrate courageous behavior. Could you use the two interchangeably? I suppose so, but in order to be brave, you'll have to tap into that courage that resides inside your soul.

A few examples of courage for someone with anxiety are as follows:

- Accepting an invitation to a friend's birthday party even when she is the only person you know.
- Trying out for a sports team when you are afraid you won't make it.

- Going to school on a day you feel like you can't get of bed because you are anxious, afraid, and depressed.
- Smiling at someone you don't think likes you.
- Getting a driver's permit when you are deeply afraid of driving.
- Journaling your thoughts about yourself.
- Telling your parents how you are feeling.
- Trying to do something you previously failed at.
- Jumping off of a diving board.
- Petting a dog even though you are afraid of dogs.
- Trying on new clothes that might not be in the same style you are used to wearing.
- Taking a recommended AP class.
- Going to a sleep away camp.
- Reaching out to a friend you haven't talked to in a while.
- Walking into a classroom after class has already begun.
- Stating your opinion or belief to someone who has a different opinion from you.
- Admitting you are wrong.
- Admitting you need help.
- Sticking up for someone who is being bullied.
- Befriending the new kid at school.
- Apologizing.
- Asking for forgiveness.

I am sure you can think of more examples of times you were courageous. And I bet that you have more courage inside of you than you ever dreamt possible.

PARENTS

It is okay to be afraid if you are noticing signs and symptoms of anxiety or your child has an official diagnosis of anxiety. Fear is a natural response to something we don't know a lot about. I want to assure you, however, that you can navigate this experience with your child(ren).

At the end of this book, I included a resource section. There are articles, books, and more that you can refer to. Most importantly, remember that you don't have to manage this on your own.

If you happen to have financial challenges, there are resources available to you. You may have to dig for them, but your pediatrician, school counselor, or local health department should be able to provide resources for free or low-cost therapy that are available. At a minimum, work with your child on the 5Cs journaling method I explain in the book.

Another fear you may have is whether or not your child(ren) will be able to live on their own, go to college, and support themselves. Every child is unique, and the severity of their anxiety disorder may play a huge factor in the future of your child(ren), but if you get them the help they need now, their chance of having a fulfilling, joyful life will increase.

Most importantly, don't let fear of a diagnosis of a mental health issue keep you from seeking help if you have noticed any of the signs, symptoms, or behaviors I've mentioned. Action is the key to navigating anxiety. Early intervention is important and will make a difference in long-term success with overcoming anxiety.

Also note, fear can trigger anger. As you navigate parenting, you may see an escalation in reactions of anger. For example, if your child is disagreeing with you, or is telling you "no," stop for a second and think about what is triggering your anger. Chances are, it isn't the reaction from your child, but an inner fear that you are associating with a childhood trauma, not necessarily a big or significant trauma, but any trauma.

For example, when I was young, my father wanted to be on time. This was a generational demand. His parents were never late, and he did not like to be late. However, my mother, was always late. To this day, she is late for everything.

We would all be ready for church, and she would be running late. The closer it got to the time to leave to be sitting in the pew on time, the more my father's anxiety and anger rose. Yelling would ensue. We would ride to church with yelling.

To this day running late causes me anxiety. Running late triggers my memory of my father's yelling, and as a result, I began yelling at my own kids. When my kids were young, I yelled a lot because that is what I knew. I did some soul searching, and I read the book *She's Gonna Blow* by Julie Ann Barnhill.

From this book, I found out I was not alone. As parents, fear triggers emotions and often anger. The fear can be related to something from our past or something in the present.

We want the best for our children, and as a result, we fear when something is not going the way we expected or planned, or when our kids are not following our values.

Once again, we can circle back to communication. Communicate with yourself when you feel the anger rising and journal around the fear or other thoughts that are triggering anger. Make sure to communicate with your children about your values, expectations, and feelings.

Also know that your child may need additional communication when something in their life is going to change, such as you are registering them for a new program, team, tutor, or other activity. Some people need additional time to process and prepare before being thrown into a new situation or experience.

When the communication line is open, you will all be better able to handle situations that arise unexpectedly and even the day-to-day challenges that arise.

In addition to communication, you'll need some courage too. The most important gift you can give your child(ren) is the understanding that having courage doesn't mean that fear does not exist, but that you do the "thing" anyway.

We are all born with a healthy amount of fear. Anxiety will take that healthy level of fear to an extreme, and potentially unhealthy, level.

There may be times in which your child(ren) can't explain the fear or be able to recognize it as irrational, and that will make it challenging for you to help them find courage. Again, patience will come into play. I hope it doesn't feel as though I am asking too much of you. There will be days when you feel that your patience is running out. When that happens, when you begin to feel like you can't help your child anymore, that is when you will have to dig deep into your soul to find courage to move forward.

To move forward, you may need to take a moment, or a thousand, to pull your own self together and muster the courage and strength to continue this journey with your child(ren), explain that you need a bit of time to gather your thoughts. Tell them you'll be back in a little while. It is important that you care for yourself too, or you will become burned out, and when that happens, zero progress will be made.

You know the saying, "If mama ain't happy, ain't nobody happy." Well, if you as parents aren't happy and healthy, you won't be able to help your child(ren) navigate life to find happiness and mental health either.

So, pull out your badge of courage and wear it proudly as you face the challenges. Hand in hand, give yourself the gift of time by stepping away from the situation to refuel your emotional energy tank. Every now and again, check to see that the badge is still there to ensure you are able to work through the fear and worry that will naturally bubble up inside of you as you watch your child(ren) struggle.

Image

Image:// a mental picture or impression of something.

 Remember, you have been criticizing yourself for years and it hasn't worked. Try approving of yourself and see what happens.

LOUISE HAY

ANXIETY IS an intrusive monster that can make us feel inadequate. When we are anxious, we can feel out of control, lost, or not good enough. One way that anxious people cope with the loss of control is through restricting or over-indulging in food or exercise. This is, of course, not the only way we deal with anxiety. Some people try to self-medicate with illicit drugs and/or alcohol or other vices.

People react to anxiety through addictions and eating disorders, so they feel control over their lives. People with anxiety often feel they have no control over any aspect of their life. As a teen, this is especially true. You have rules at home, rules at school, you have to ask permission to do almost everything, and you are told what you have to do. You have to do chores. You have to do homework, on and on. Then, if you have constant thoughts that you can't seem to get in check, you may feel a sense of desperation to control something, anything.

I have not had experience with drugs. Thankfully, I never allowed myself to try them out of fear of addiction (some fear is good fear). I did, however, struggle with an eating disorder. It began in high school. I was always told I was not fat, just big boned. Who wants to be big anything? I didn't, and the older I got the more my anxiety increased and the more I needed something to control. I loved to eat and was always active, but I didn't like how I looked. My body and what I put into it were things I could control. No one else had control over these things. Sure, I was told to come to dinner, but no one put food in my mouth, or monitored what or how much I ate or exercised.

My eating disorder started with making myself vomit after meals. This didn't last long as I hated vomiting and wasn't very good at making myself do it. I won't classify myself as bulimic because I never gorged myself and then purged. I purged what I ate after meals, usually only in the evenings.

When I went to college, I gained the traditional freshman fifteen (fifteen pounds from eating all of the fried dorm food and drinking beer at parties—a bad combination for the waistline). At one point during the year, I went home, and my grandmother said to me "where did my doll girl go?" This was her way of letting me know that I had put on too much weight. This was my indication that I needed to get the weight off. When I went home for the summer, I started walking, running, and limiting my food intake so that I could lose the weight. And I did. I dropped a recognizable amount.

This food limiting and exercise regimen continued into my second year of college and lasted beyond graduation. By my fifth year of school, I was limiting my food intake to a 1,000 calories per day. I ran six plus miles, did aerobics, and always took the stairs instead of elevators to burn those calories. I had my diet down to a science, permitting myself a certain number of M&Ms, my favorite candy, a day. At that point, I wasn't going home often, but when I did, my mother always told me I was too thin. She wanted me to eat more. She and my daddy had no idea how much I was running or how little I was eating. At most I saw them once a month. Every time I did see them, they commented on how I looked. To give perspective, I weighed 115 pounds and 5'7.5" tall, (with big bones).

Was I thin? Not in my eyes. At that point in my life, I thought I was fat. I hated my body, and everything about it. I wore baggy clothes most of the time so no one could see my body. Thankfully, it was the late 80's and early '90s, and shoulder pads were a real thing. I could hide my body for the most part.

My mom would point out that she could see or feel my bones. I would disagree. When asked about eating, I would say I did eat, and I was just stressed. I had a lot of excuses for her. I did eat when I was with her, but not much, and I made sure I burned the calories off. Looking back, I realize how sick I was. I did go to a few group therapy sessions for patients with eating disorders, but other than that, I was simply blessed that my mom prayed a lot, and I eventually overcame my eating disorder without requiring medical intervention.

It has taken me years (YEARS!) to be able to look in the mirror and find something I liked about my body. I exercise now, to stay healthy, strong and lean, but am not obsessed with the need to burn off calories consumed. I still see more flaws than positives but have learned through a lot of therapy and grace from God to accept my body as a healthy machine that is working and doing its job every day. Eating is something I now enjoy, but I make healthy choices (most of the time) and *never* diet. Trust me, it is very hard not to get sucked into the latest and greatest diet schemes I see advertised on social media. There will probably always be triggers for me, but I know that I have to stay healthy to be here for my children, so I work hard at avoiding the triggers and focusing on the gifts of my body and its functions.

When I refer to triggers, I am really speaking about stress or lack of control in my circumstances. For example, when I feel stressed or sad, I will still fall back on limiting food; I simply have no appetite. When my father was fighting cancer, I didn't want to eat. In fact, I couldn't eat. I fell back into the pattern of controlling what I could control. Some people eat more when stressed; I eat less. Both can be problematic, and this is why we need to prevent ourselves from going down a path that can ultimately harm our bodies.

Another thing I avoid, except for my annual physical exams, is the scale. The scale can be our worst enemy if we are struggling with an eating disorder. If we have a medical condition like diabetes or heart disease and are told we need to lose weight in order to live, then yes, a scale can be an effective tool. Likewise, if we are overcoming an eating disorder, it is important to do weight checks to ensure our bodies are getting the nutrition they need. For the most part, for those of us with eating disorders, the scale is not our friend, and it is best to avoid it. You can gauge your body by how your clothes fit. You do not need a number to define you unless, of course, you are under a doctor's care.

When I look back at that time in my life, I was more than twenty-five pounds lighter than I am now. I now see what my mom saw, but there was no convincing me then. Embrace your body, and if you cannot, seek help. The longer you spend hating your body, limiting food, gorging and purging, or exercising at extreme lengths of time, the harder it will be to overcome an eating disorder. If someone tells you you are looking too thin, take that as a cue to get help.

I realize I make this sound easy. It isn't, I know. But, if you notice that you are analyzing your body, thinking you are fat, have altered your eating patterns, are gorging and purging, or even tempted to, it is time to seek help.

Eating disorders are no joke. I know women who have serious health issues from the years they spent living with an eating disorder. Unfortunately, I also know people who have been hospitalized numerous times because their bodies couldn't thrive without proper nutrition. Sadly, a couple of them passed away.

A diagnosis of an eating disorder may or may not be a choice, but you do have a choice to seek and accept help before it gets out of hand and influences the rest of your life. Again, this sounds easy but may not be. Remember, your brain is not working properly if you have an eating disorder. The messaging in your brain is confused and may not be capable of allowing you to make the decisions you know are best for you. You might think: *One more day. If I'm not better in one more day, I'll get help.* But that day will come, and then another and another. You need to find someone you trust and let them in to support you. You might feel angry at them when they suggest you get help. You might even hate them for making you get help. Know they have your best interest at heart, and they will ultimately be saving your life.

The digital era has created a very skewed view on body image. No one, and I mean no one, is perfect. Perfection is a myth. It is unachievable.

Some girls and women are blessed with amazing bodies, but chances are, there are other things they struggle with. No one has it all, and it is best to focus on the parts of you that you are confident about, and not focus on what others have or seem to be. Comparing yourself with others is a path to misery. This is where gratitude comes in. Make a list of all of the things your mind and body can do well. Each one is a blessing to be grateful for. When you start to compare yourself to others, focusing on your flaws, refer to this list and let gratitude come over you as a blanket of peace.

If you're able to do so, look in a mirror. Yes, now. Look at your eyes. Take in the color of them. Take in your own soul. You can see your soul through your eyes, and others see you through those gorgeous soulful eyes you are carrying around on that perfectly imperfect body of yours.

Self-care can make a huge difference in how you feel about yourself. Take time to shower every day. Brush your teeth and hair, wash your face, put lotion on your body, and cream on your face. Gently touch your skin, and when you do, remind yourself that every inch of you is worthy, no matter the weight or height.

There are some amazing examples in the world today to inspire you to accept your body as it is. I know this is difficult. I know this is a huge challenge if you are struggling with body image. I know that if you are struggling at the moment you might be thinking, "Whatever, Robyn, you have no idea how fat and ugly I am." Guess what? I do because I was once there, feeling those same feelings, and it has taken me years to feel somewhat secure in my own skin. I wasted a lot of energy being negative and not loving myself. This is your opportunity to recognize your thoughts and seek help if they are not healthy. No one needs to know you are in therapy. No one needs to know you have an eating disorder. This is your journey, and as long as you take the right steps to put yourself on the path to health, no one will judge you.

Here's the thing: You will never be able to accept love from others until you accept and love yourself. Likewise, you will not be able to love and care for others until you love yourself. God gave you one body. Appreciate it, respect yourself, and don't waste the time I wasted hating my body and image. Your life will take a turn for the better when you decide to accept yourself as you were beautifully made.

Seeing a nutritionist is beneficial for all types of eating disorders. In addition, exercise is key to a healthy lifestyle. Again, this is something you want to work through with a therapist or your doctor, depending on your eating disorder. Your individual exercise plan should be determined alongside an adult who can guide you and ensure you don't over- or under-do it.

> Talk to yourself the way you would talk to your best friend, someone you love. You would not tell your best friend that she is ugly or fat. Self-acceptance begins with being kind to yourself.

PARENTS

Image is a tough one! Here are the two best pieces of advice I can give you:

1. Be present and observe your child(ren). It is important to have a good idea of what their daily habits are, so that if there is a dramatic change, which may build over time, you catch it sooner than later. If you notice they are picking at their food and eating less and less over time, you may want to monitor more closely and discuss your observation with her. An increase in exercise duration and frequency is another alarm bell. If you notice both together, start the conversations with your child(ren) but don't wait to get help. It can take weeks to get into a therapist, so the earlier you act, the earlier your child(ren) will have the help they need and the better the chances for full recovery. Another

sign to watch for is a change in wardrobe. If suddenly, they are wearing baggy clothing, they may be trying to hide their body. Or, maybe they don't want to wear a bathing suit in front of others. Either way, observe and have a conversation to determine if intervention is necessary.
2. Do not talk about your weight, your own body image issues, or dieting in front of your children. Children are naturally curious, and they listen to and watch everything we say and do. If your child(ren) hears you complaining about your body, they are naturally going to think twice about their own body, especially if you are fit, or of average height and weight.

I told the story about my eating disorder. To this day, my sisters and I have significant body image issues. I worked so incredibly hard to overcome my eating disorder, and I honestly can't say that I have completely. This is a lifelong struggle for me; however, I have learned how to navigate it and recognize when I am going down the wrong path.

When my sisters and I were young, everyone talked about their weight and dieting. If you grew up in the seventies and eighties, I am sure you can relate. My grandmothers, aunts, mother, and her friends were always talking about eating less, limiting calories, and exercising more. So were some of my friends' mothers. Naturally, we took this all in, and as we read magazines, we saw nothing but thin, beautiful women, and read about the latest and greatest diet fads or ways to lose weight.

My grandmother even had a machine that you stood on, wrapped a canvas belt around you, and as the machine shook the fat, like it was supposed to melt off you. The gimmicks! Silliness!

It isn't any different today except now your child(ren) are not only hearing this from people around them but seeing it on social media. They see the keto diet, cleanses, intermittent fasting, no sugar, no carbs, and the list goes on!

The only thing that will keep your child(ren) healthy is a healthy lifestyle: Eating healthy, organic (when possible) foods and moderate exercise. Everything in moderation is the key.

If you eat healthy and exercise, you will be the example your child(ren) needs. If you happen to have a health crisis or make the decision to lose weight by dieting, be discreet about the details and have the conversation with your child(ren) about the importance of getting healthy. The emphasis should not be on the number on the scale, but on a healthy, balanced lifestyle.

My husband and I have always had alcohol in our home. We enjoy wine, beer or the occasional cocktail, and I'll never turn down a glass of champagne. Our philosophy has been that the more we demonstrate a healthy relationship with alcohol and have conversations about moderation with our children, the better the chances will be that they make similar choices as they approach their adult years.

The same with food choices. I love dessert and so does my husband. I love to bake, and I love to see my children light up when I make my special triple chip cookies, scones or cinnamon rolls for them. I never eliminated those things from our diet because I wanted them to learn to eat the treats in moderation while also enjoying healthy choices.

Have I done it all perfectly? No. I've had to work extra hard and have made many food mistakes. I've also exposed my children to my thoughts. Fortunately, to date, we've all come through it okay, and have a genuine appreciation for food, meals together, and traditions in the kitchen.

Speaking of meals together: one thing that will help your child(ren) more than almost anything, is connecting as a family at mealtime. Having family dinners is an excellent way to stay connected and check in. Having daily dinners together has always been a priority in our family. Even if we had sports in the evening, we would have dinner together and then have a snack, if need be, depending on the timing of everything. It became an expectation, and one we have always enjoyed, even when times were stressful and no one really had the time to take. We at least had five or ten minutes to connect, say our dinner prayers, and be present for each other.

Shame was the topic of a previous chapter, and it also applies to body image and food. If your child(ren) is already struggling with anxiety, putting emphasis on their outward appearance or weight may not help them, and could cause them to feel shame. Listen, I have no filter so things like this are challenging for me. My son used to get so frustrated with me. We laugh about it now, but if his skin was breaking out, I would inevitably notice at dinner when he was sitting next to me, and I would say something. Even my husband would remind me to shush on the subject. Of course, I didn't do it to make him feel badly. I wanted to remind him to use his medicine and wash his face after practice. However, it wasn't the right time, and he already knew he was having a breakout, so my input wasn't of value.

I tell you this so that if you make the same mistake and say something you wish you hadn't, apologize. Don't feel shame but also have the conversation with your child(ren) to ensure she doesn't feel shame about her appearance either.

Relationships

Relationship:// the way in which two or more people are connected.

> In all the world there is no heart for me like yours. In all the world there is no love for you like mine.
>
> MAYA ANGELOU

LOOK at relationships with family and friends as necessities. We all need someone to love and someone to love us, but not at the expense of falling away from your values, morals, integrity, or losing your sense of self. Make a list your non-negotiables when it comes to relationships. These non-negotiables will help you make good decisions when it comes to choosing friends and your romantic relationships. We can't choose our family, but we can choose how we treat others and what we tolerate from others. Here are some of my non-negotiables that help me stay grounded in my relationships with friends and family members:

- Upholding my values
- Having integrity
- Being kind

- Being honest
- Living with empathy
- Being compassionate
- Walking in my faith
- Surrounding myself with positive people
- Protecting my body
- Staying healthy
- Getting enough sleep
- Journaling
- Daily devotions
- Prioritizing family
- Trust
- Integrity
- Forgiving myself and others for mistakes
- Focusing on daily gratitude

My Non-Negotiables	Why This is Non-Negotiable
Honesty	I want people to trust me
Faith	It gives me hope, comfort, and peace
Being thoughtful	I want others to know I care about them
Getting enough sleep	I don't want to be crabby because I'm tired

NAVIGATING RELATIONSHIPS

No other human being will make you whole, worthy, confident, beautiful, or better. Being able to have and maintain relationships begins with your relationship with yourself. We will dive deeper into this in future chapters, but it is important for you to recognize it before we talk about relationships. How you treat yourself will influence how you treat others. When talking to yourself, do not say anything that you would not say to your best friend. When you are kind to yourself, you will be able to be more open-minded with and kind to others.

Having and maintaining relationships might be the most challenging part of life for people with anxiety. I said it before, and I'll say it again, anxiety leads to anger, shame, fear, and self-doubt. Think about those words for a minute. They are in complete contrast to joy, love, and trust. Which list of words do you think are going to help maintain better relationships? You guessed it: Joy, love, and trust. But, when you have anxiety, those three emotions are much harder to feel and much harder to attain because of the self-doubt that accompanies anxiety. The brain is constantly questioning everything we say and do, and everything others say and do. This makes it is harder to accept and please ourselves. This may lead to pushing others away.

Pushing others away will result in failed relationships. Communication, or lack thereof, is also a common cause of failed relationships. The two go hand in hand. If you aren't communicating effectively and sharing how you feel, either good or bad, you may push people away.

Similarly, if you are always trying to please others by going along with what they want, agreeing with their opinions, or suppressing your true feelings and beliefs, you may become frustrated and resentful over time. When frustration and resentment build within relationships, it's hard to maintain positive energy, and continue to be kind and patient. This tends to happen especially when one feels taken advantage of and disrespected time after time.

What is communication? What does it mean to have good communication?

Communication is sharing information, feelings, experiences, and emotions. As humans, we can communicate verbally and non-verbally. A smile is a form of non-verbal communication. Verbal communication is sharing your thoughts, feelings, emotions, or experiences with someone else in a conversation or in writing. Speaking about emotions and certain life experiences can be challenging; therefore, some people prefer to write about them. Communication is generally two ways, telling someone something and that person responding to what you've shared.

Good communication involves both listening and sharing. We cannot truly communicate if we aren't willing to listen. Listening isn't just hearing what someone else is saying. It is connecting with the words being said, observing emotions while they speak, not letting your focus dissipate as they share, and responding accordingly. It is not cutting someone off in the middle of their sentence, letting distractions pull you away from the person sharing, or saying you know how they feel without having experienced what they are describing.

Communication isn't always with other people. We communicate with ourselves too. Our mind and body communicate to help us identify emotions such as fear, anxiety, sadness, anger and more. It's just as important to listen to your body and mind as it is to listen during a conversation with a friend.

Deep connection in relationships begins with communication. We should feel comfortable sharing about feelings, dreams, goals, and experiences with those who have earned trust to hear and hold them safely for us.

Remember when you were younger, and your teacher would fill a jar with cotton balls, marbles, or wooden sticks when the class behaved well? When the jar was full, the class was rewarded with a pajama party, movie, or treats. Brené Brown uses this as an example of friendship. Your teacher might have removed items when behavior wasn't on par with her expectations. Then, it took longer to get the reward.

You can use this same example with building relationships. You don't have to have an actual jar to put things in, but you can monitor your feelings and thoughts around people. Recognize and keep track of those thoughts and feelings for how well you trust someone. What does your gut say?

Intuition is a powerful tool within our bodies and mind to guide us on whether we can trust someone. Follow those instincts. When you believe people have earned your trust, spill the beans. Before then, be cautious to avoid hurt and worry over someone else holding your truths and sharing them without your permission.

Sharing emotions and feelings can be hard. I encourage you to be open and honest. If your parents demonstrate they care for you, and ask you how you feel or what's wrong, tell them what's going on so they can give you guidance.

Even though it is hard, it's better to share feelings and emotions. Bottling them up inside can create more anxiety. Share your feelings and emotions with those you trust, and don't attempt to stifle the emotions of someone else either. Hiding emotions and not being honest with feelings are what causes strife in relationships. The more strife in your relationships, the more anxiety you will carry around with you.

A side note: If you don't tell you parents about how you are feeling, they may worry, get upset, or think you are hiding something. They may continue to ask you what's wrong, and they are likely to assume the worst. You don't have to tell them every little detail about how you feel or why but share that you are feeling sad. Maybe explain that you need to let the feelings come over you and go away, and then you'll be able to tell them about it. Ask for their patience, but let them know you are working through it, and they don't need to worry. Hiding your emotions or showing them without explaining what's wrong, may cause tension between you and your parents.

If your parents know you are okay, and you are working through your emotions, they'll most likely be willing to wait for you to come to them if you need them. The important thing is for the two parties to communicate that to each other.

> If having conversations is difficult, write your thoughts and feelings in the form of a note to your parents. Verbal communication isn't always easy or available to people with anxiety. In that instance, written communication is always an option.

There are some families where communication isn't a priority, and this can lead to long-term animosity and a breakdown in family dynamics. If you are struggling to communicate with your parents, talk to a guidance counselor, or ask your parents to help you find a therapist. Maybe you can go to therapy as a family to navigate the needs of everyone involved.

Sometimes a third party is needed to break the ice, release the tension, open the line of communication, and provide suggestions on how you can work together to communicate effectively.

It's important to note that it is completely normal for people with anxiety to have feelings and emotions that they can't describe or explain. It takes time sitting with yourself and thinking about the events of the day. This helps you figure out the trigger that set off your emotions. Just like asking your parents to be patient with you while you work through your feelings, be patient with yourself. But do the work of focusing on what is happening with your feelings and what could have caused it. Was it something you saw, something you read, something someone said to you, something someone did to you, something you said, or something you did? Note that if you have experienced trauma, a memory could have stimulated the emotions you are feeling. Post-traumatic stress often causes severe anxiety.

Let's call these things triggers. They are triggering an emotion or feeling that you don't like or aren't comfortable with. Track them and if you can identify where they begin, you can start avoiding them, challenging them, or changing them. This will help you spend more time in a neutral or happy place of feeling instead of feeling sad, anxious, angry, or frustrated or even from lashing out at others.

Doing this exercise will help you identify the emotions earlier in the process and help you navigate that emotion going forward.

What I'm Feeling	When Did the Feeling Start	What Was the Trigger
My stomach hurts	This morning	Geometry test
Tired	I couldn't sleep last night	Presentation

Once you have written about the feelings and triggers, journal around them. Writing can be very therapeutic and help you create a strategy for avoiding triggers in the future or react to or handle them more pleasantly.

IT'S TIME TO SPEAK UP—THINK SELF-ADVOCACY

Sometimes relationships feel one-sided. There may be people in your life who make you feel that you don't matter. That your voice, opinion, maybe even your presence, doesn't matter. The person or people making you feel this way may not even realize that they are doing so. Unfortunately, people get very wrapped up in their own worlds, and neglect to think of others or realize they are making others feel less worthy or unloved.

This can hurt. And it can also make you feel more anxious, especially when around such people.

Self-worth. It comes from within, not from outside. You have the power and authority to believe you are worthy. No one else can determine your worth.

Your worth is not attached to what you can do, who you are friends with, how smart you are, what you weigh, how long your hair is, your family's income, or how many friends you have. Yes, others can cause you to feel less or more worthy, but the power to feel worthy comes your belief in yourself, knowing you have a valuable place in this world.

People can hurt you, put you down, damage your spirit, make you feel less secure or feel less worthy. You have a choice, though, to permit them to influence how you feel about yourself. Often, they are damaging your spirit because their spirit has been damaged by someone. They are probably struggling, hurting, and feeling unworthy.

These are very difficult situations. You may start to really dislike the person for making you feel this way while feeling down about yourself. Or, you may try to please them by sacrificing your own beliefs and joy to make them feel better. You may work really hard to try to get them to accept you and think you are good enough.

None of this is optimal. If possible, choose to separate yourself from anyone who makes you feel negative about yourself. If the people making you feel this way live in your household, you may not have a choice but to put up with their hurtful behaviors and comments. But you do have a choice in how you let their words and actions make you feel. Decide you are worthy, you are a gift from above, and have value to add to this world.

If you are feeling self-doubt, unworthiness, or a lack of self-esteem, I encourage you to journal about these thoughts and feelings. Put sticky notes on your mirror or bedroom door and remind yourself daily that you are worthy of love and acceptance.

Look in the mirror and say out loud, "I love you. You are worthy. You are beautiful. You are smart. You are kind. You are valuable." Such affirmations will transform your mindset and confidence level.

God placed you here on earth, and no matter what, you will have worth in His eyes. He has plans for you and that alone makes you worthy.

Anxiety often prevents us from saying what we feel (good or bad), standing up for ourselves, or speaking our truth. It is all related to a lack of confidence and trust in ourselves. People with anxiety often become doormats; they let other people step all over them because they don't speak up for themselves.

Doing the aforementioned activities to improve your self-worth, self-esteem, and self-confidence will help prevent people from taking advantage of you or treating you poorly. It may take a lot of courage to speak up and stand up for yourself, but the more you journal around your self-worth and believe it, the more strength and courage you will have.

When we don't speak up for ourselves, we can be sucked into abusive relationships or in a place of unhappiness, always doing what other people want us to do. Once in the rut of not speaking up for ourselves, we are at risk of losing our voices.

Speaking up for yourself doesn't mean being rude, hateful, or talking back to others. Yes, they are going to frustrate and annoy you, and not "get" you, but it is your responsibility to treat them with kindness and respect.

Speaking up for yourself means saying "no" when you don't want to do what someone else suggests. It can also mean suggesting an alternative or coming up with a compromise. Doormats always say yes, go along with what everyone else wants, and end up feeling down, bad, or anxious.

What you want to avoid is being a people pleaser at the expense of losing yourself. When you try to please others by submerging your feelings and desires, not stating your opinions, and just going along with what they want, you sacrifice yourself and squelch your desires. The more you sacrifice yourself, the further in the rut of negative self-talk, frustration, overwhelm, anxiety, anger, and shame you will fall into.

Likewise, if you love, respect, and cherish someone, tell them. If they aren't clear on how you feel about them, they may not stick around to support you, love you, and hang out with you. And, if you have a problem with someone, tell them kindly. Don't tell someone else and talk about the person behind their back; speak directly to the person and address the issue. This will save anxiety and unnecessary hurt feelings and stress. Gossip and talking about others behind their backs are never the solutions. Hurt causes hurt. Lies lead to more lies. Gossip leads to the ruin of relationships and broken hearts. It is always best to communicate your feelings and needs directly to the person affecting you and influencing your feelings.

Again, this isn't easy, whether it is your parents, friends, or teammates, but trust me on this one. If you go straight to the source, it will save you a lot of anxiety and heartache going forward. Tap into your courage now and learn these communication skills. You will be saved a lot of grief and time in your future. If speaking to someone is too intimidating at first, write them a note. Then, next time, try to speak instead of writing. Maybe you will always have to write, but at least you are expressing how you feel or what you want from your relationship with them.

I didn't learn how to stop being a people pleaser until recently. I've always agreed with everyone on almost everything because I was afraid to rock the boat, or be judged for my opinions or desires, or hurt someone's feelings. I sacrificed myself for the sake of others. There is always room for compromise, and we always have the right to state our opinions, thoughts, desires, and needs.

What other people think and say about you is out of your control. If you don't want to feel like a doormat, you have to be willing to speak up for yourself and ensure you are pleased to protect your own mental health.

Use your voice to share ideas, say yes or no, speak up, and share your opinion. I was always afraid people wouldn't like me or would think I was weird, so I didn't speak up. In hindsight, there are many scenarios I wish I had voiced my opinion because the outcome would have been different.

Speaking up takes practice, and you have to tap into your courage. As you tap into your courage, make sure you speak according to your values when it comes to relationships.

Sometimes people with anxiety who lack confidence will seek love in the wrong ways from the wrong people. Physical attraction is one thing but giving yourself to someone just to have them "love" you or accept you is going to end in disaster. You will feel less worthy and more shameful.

Remember that you are a person with heart and purpose, and your values should drive you toward that purpose.

 Jealousy is the result of one's lack of self-confidence, self-worth, and self-acceptance.

SASHA AZEVEDO

As you forge relationships, you may have to deal with jealousy. In my opinion, jealousy is a root of evil.

It's not a good idea to look at someone else and think their life is better than yours. The grass is almost never greener on the other side of the fence, and there are always skeletons that haven't been let out of closets. It's also not a good idea to let jealousy influence how you feel or treat another person. Likewise, be prepared to watch for jealousy in relationships. As humans it's fairly common to seek more, want more, or want what others have. If there is turmoil in one of your relationships, see if you've had some great things happen to you that could cause jealousy. This happens, unfortunately. It's sad that we can't be happy for others, but it's a reality. I wouldn't recommend accusing someone of being jealous, but if you feel this is happening, be extra kind to the person. Let them know your success doesn't change the friendship and that you are there to support them no matter what is happening in their life or yours.

When people are jealous because they've seen you rising above and doing the right things, they may put you down. If this happens, they may not be your people. It's important to choose to be with people who are going to support you and make you feel good about yourself. You want to be around people whom you want to support and love, too. Positive energy is important for everyone but especially those of us with anxiety. Negative energy can amplify anxiety, insecurities, and a lack of self-esteem.

Energy creates energy. Energy is contagious, positive and negative. You get to choose the energy you want to catch and spread.

How do I know that? Because when you are living for good, when you are loving yourself, when you are living your purpose, when you are following God's plan, you are doing bigger things and are being the bigger person. Live by your values. Hold true to your morals and integrity. You don't need any other human to make you whole or worthy, confident or beautiful.

Now, the reality is, it hurts. It hurts deep. It burns like a fire climbing up your arm and approaching your neck. Insults strike a flame of fear, especially if you have a tender heart. You are going to get hurt, but that is a beautiful thing because if you weren't hurting, you would be callous and angry, and those emotions won't get you anywhere pleasant. Try to take the high road, the path harder to travel, and always be the bigger-better person.

Remember we never really know where people are coming from. They may be coming from a really dark place so let the hurt be present for a moment, and then, stand up tall and march forward to the place you can continue to serve and follow your purpose. Do not, DO NOT, let other people stop you from being the best version of you. Do the next right thing: Be kind, forgive, support the positive people, and bless and release those who bring negative energy that doesn't fuel your soul.

One of the most dangerous things you can do is to depend on the opinions of others. If you make your decisions based on what other people think, every person in your life has control over your choices and your behaviors. This is similar to people-pleasing—when we constantly live to please others or let others make decisions for us. Deciding to follow your gut instinct (intuition) and making decisions that align with your values and morals, are the first steps in moving toward claiming yourself and owning your decisions as the person God is calling you to be. That may sound peculiar. Is God calling you to be someone now, as a teen? Yes. He's got a plan for you, and in that plan, there are people He wants you to serve, help, and love. Sometimes, blessing and releasing those who make you feel less than worthy is helping them too.

When you walk into a room, you have the right to be who you are and who you were meant to be. You have the right to express yourself and your beliefs, in a kind and loving way. If others who care about you and love you are going to give you their opinions, take their opinions with a grain of salt. You can do whatever you dream of doing. Why should their negative opinion be allowed to determine whether or not you follow your dreams? You will experience more harm by not living the life you dream of because of fear of others' opinions, than you will ever experience by following your dreams and being your authentic self.

Please note that this is not permission to do whatever you want despite your parents' warning that it is not safe or healthy. They have lived and probably experienced, to some extent, everything you are experiencing socially. They just might know a thing or two more than you about what is best for you. When I say follow your dreams and share your opinions, this recommendation is made from a place of remaining kind, respectful, safe, and be responsible. I am coming from the place of wanting you to know that you are worthy and that you have the right to stand up for yourself—without another human degrading you or taking away your rights to express yourself.

THE NEXT RIGHT THING

God has given you purpose, and you will feel little nudges from Him guiding you. His plan for you is mapped out, but he's also given you free will to make your own decisions. It's a powerful gift and one that must be treated with respect. Therefore, when making decisions, ask yourself, "What is the next right thing and how will my decision align with my values and morals?" Ask yourself how the next decision you make will affect you or anyone else around you. If there is the possibility for harm or hurt feelings, it may not be the next right thing, or maybe there is a compromise available that would protect you and others from any harm.

Relationships can be the most beautiful thing on earth, but they can also be one of the most detrimental. Be true to your values first, then, work to serve others. But serve them in ways that you know would be pleasing to God, will keep you safe, and align with your morals and values. Serve in ways that are healthy for you, both physically and emotionally.

 They may forget what you said, but they will never forget how you made them feel.

CARL W. BUEHNER

Be humble, kind, and gracious. When pride or arrogance slip into your mindset and behavior patterns, trouble will follow in relationships and everything in life. Be open to learning and be curious. Curiosity can fuel a lot of conversations and help you build relationships that are strong and secure.

Be intentional. Don't just do or say to be doing or saying. Be intentional with your thoughts, what you say, and with your actions. Setting intentions is a powerful tool for overcoming obstacles and achieving goals. If you set intentions for your relationships and how you will treat others and yourself, you will have better experiences and less anxiety or worry about your relationships.

Remember, words matter. What you say and how you say it will influence the thoughts and feelings of others. Likewise, what you say to yourself matters. Choose your words wisely and with positive intentions no matter who you are speaking to.

Be mindful. Don't let other people's chaos be your chaos. When that negative energy becomes too much, it's okay to remove yourself from it. Everything in life comes down to choices. You should be able to feel confident in each of those choices if you make your decisions based on the next right thing.

SEX

Did I just hear you giggle? I know sex can feel like an awkward topic. But I feel it's one that has to be addressed because as your body changes, your anxiety may shift.

Straight out of the gate I want you to know that having sex before you are ready can increase anxiety. You are a teenager and that means your body is changing, your emotions may be stronger than ever before, and you may feel the need for others' approval. There will be opportunities to date and possibly fall in love.

You might experience relationships where the person you are dating wants to have sex. They might say to you, "If you love me, you'll have sex with me." Or they might give you an ultimatum like, "If we don't have sex, I'm going to break up with you."

Think about letting this person go. They're demonstrating behavior that shows they doesn't respect your decisions. If you aren't ready, the pressure may trigger your anxiety.

Did you know that the brain does not fully develop until you are twenty-five years old? Girls mature much faster than boys, so know boys may not be ready for long-term commitments or mature decision-making until much later than you. This is something to think about if you are having sex because he may not be ready for the responsibility of having a child should you become pregnant.

Sex can add complications. If you are an anxious person and you start having sex, now you have a "what if" about getting pregnant. Every month you'll be counting the minutes until your cycle starts. You'll need to focus on schoolwork, but you'll be unable to because you'll be worried that you are pregnant. You'll become irritable, frustrated, angry, and overwhelmed. You might not get the A you want because you'll be too anxious to do the work that needs to be done to earn it.

And, as a pharmacist, I want to remind you that birth control pills are not 100 percent effective. Neither are condoms. The pull-out method a guy may try to convince you is safe is not effective either.

I understand raging hormones; I had them too! I think everyone I know had them. And I understand the desire to please someone and the feeling that if you have sex with them, they'll by yours forever. But life doesn't work that way. Each time you give yourself to someone, you lose part of yourself, and they take that piece of you with them. You can't get it back.

Think of it like this. If you have sex with someone at sixteen, and you date for a year or two, and then break up when you leave for college, you'll start dating again. You could have a plethora of boyfriends by the time you graduate college. If you have sex with several people by the time you graduate college, you will have given a piece of yourself to each of them that you won't be able to give to the person you marry. Your one true love. And worse, there is a risk of comparison and jealousy in that relationship. I'm sure it seems silly to think about now. I don't want to be preachy, but I do want you to be aware that sex is serious business with potential risks, complications, and added stress and anxiety.

Another thought: If you are looking for love and security, having sex is not going to fulfill that need, at least not permanently.

I recognize the societal norms, that sex is commonplace, and everyone does it. I encourage you to think differently. Sex is sex, but making love is a bond between two people that is meant to bring you together as one. When you truly love someone, you are sharing your whole self with them. It's meaningful. It's not a one-off thing that you just do to do. Sex wasn't designed to be a recreational activity between people who aren't in love. I think this concept goes hand in hand with respecting and loving your body. You don't need to have sex to feel loved. Oh, it might feel good, no matter what, but after it's over, you are left with the worry and anxiety of the questions that will likely spin a web in your mind. Thoughts and questions like:

- Was I good enough?
- Does he love me?
- What if I get pregnant?
- Oh God, please don't let me get pregnant.
- My parents will kill me if I get pregnant.
- What if I have to give up college?
- What if I contracted an STD?
- Oh phew, I got my period. It only lasted a day, oh no! Am I pregnant?
- He's talking to that girl so he likes her more.
- Oh no! He's going to break up with me.
- I better have more sex with this person.
- What is he saying to them, they keep looking at me?

These and more thoughts may roll through your head. Meanwhile, most likely, they'll be out hanging with their buddies and going about their business without a second thought. I caution you to think twice if you don't want the escalation in your anxious thoughts.

I also want to encourage you to realize that you don't have to have sex to be accepted and loved. You don't have to give yourself away and increase your anxiety to be liked and have relationships. Someday you may want to get married, and if you think about your partner having had multiple partners before you, you'll start wondering if you're as good as the others, if your partner likes you as much as they liked them, if you please your partner the way the others did. The wondering and comparison results in more anxiety and maybe arguments, and ultimately, a relationship that might not last.

You might not want to wait until you are married, I totally get that, but I do suggest that you wait until you are out of high school. In the long run, you may experience more joy if you wait until you are more mature and can make the best decisions for your body and care for a child should you become pregnant. Not to mention, if you have dreams and aspirations for your future, having sex in high school could prevent opportunities or complicate your future should you become pregnant.

It is really none of my business whether you have sex or not. But I know how anxiety can influence day-to-day life, and if I can save you from additional stress and anxiety, I would love to do so.

In my opinion, abortion is wrong, that when the sperm and egg come together, a baby is formed. I was only six weeks pregnant when I saw the heart beats of both my sons. I saw life.

God designed this miraculous event, sex, to procreate, and even though there are only a few cells at first, those cells are the beginning of a life, a life that will grow for nine months inside of you and become a human for you to love and care for.

Do I know people that have had abortions? Yes. Would I ever judge them? No, never because I wasn't in their shoes. But what I want to stress to you is that having an abortion didn't solve their "problem." It made life easier for the time being, but it left a burden on their hearts, a lifelong burden. For years, they struggled with guilt, shame, and anxiety over the decision they made. These weren't feelings anyone else put on them; they were feelings they felt on their own.

This has nothing to do with politics. Abortion might seem like the best decision. You have to weigh the benefits and consequences of increased anxiety, and so many other emotions you may be left with. The best thing to do is to try your best to make good decisions every day. Protect your body and mind, by making decisions that are age-appropriate and ensure you are ready to handle any circumstance that arises from your actions.

Adoption is something to consider if you become pregnant. I know so many people who ache to have a baby but cannot. They are seeking to adopt, but resources and babies are limited. If you are not ready to raise a child and you become pregnant, consider a match adoption program where you can choose the parents for your child, and give the child a chance at life and an opportunity to fill another person's life with joy. You would have to sacrifice nine months of your life, but you would be giving life to another human and filling another family with joy.

I know it is not easy. I didn't always want to wait either. My advantage was that I did not want to be a teen mom like my mom, and I was afraid of punishment and disappointing my parents. Looking back, even when I did have sex for the first time, I wish I hadn't, and I wish it hadn't been with who it was with. I can't say I didn't know better at the time. I did. My conscience was telling me one thing, but social pressure told me something different. I decided to follow social pressure and ultimatums from the guy I was dating.

The last thought I want to leave you with relating to sex this this: Protect yourself. I recently read a story about a young girl who met a guy, dated for a few weeks, had sex, broke up, and she was left with herpes. She was uncomfortable, in pain, and felt disgusting. Now she doesn't have a choice but to live with the possibility of future outbreaks, and she has to tell all of her future partners that she has herpes. Another opportunity for anxiety to soar! Can you imagine the stress and embarrassment of having to tell someone you care about that you have an STD and just hope they won't leave you?

> Don't rush to grow up! You have the rest of your life to have sex and intimate relationships. Be a kid while you have the chance to be a kid! Time is fleeting and before

you know it all the adult responsibilities of a job and life will be in your lap. Enjoy youth while it is yours to enjoy!

WORK HARD AND LOVE HARDER

Remember, it's going to hurt like crazy when you lose someone, but it is worth the pain if you've been blessed to experience love. I believe it's better to have loved and lost than to have not loved at all. Don't let fear and anxiety hold you back from building relationships, friendships, or other. People have so much to offer us, and love can be so fulfilling and such a beautiful blessing.

∼

PARENTS

Do you remember being a teen and navigating relationships? It wasn't easy, and I believe it's even harder for our children. Social media and the additional social pressures add a new layer of stress and risk of anxiety.

I stated a lot throughout this chapter; some of which you may agree with and some that you may disagree with. At the end of the day, the important thing is for you to be there for your child(ren), to support them when they are experiencing challenges within their relationships, handling social pressures, and trying to make the right decisions.

Relationships can be very complex. I focused more on the friendship and dating aspect of relationships because I believe they are the hardest to work through during teen years. My goal was to help your child(ren) find her voice, to stand up for herself, and not let anxiety hold her back from having healthy relationships. Also, I wanted to teach them to stand up for themselves and their desires for their lives and bodies.

We may differ in opinions when it comes to sex and abortion, and that is fine. My goal for including these topics was to give teenagers guidance when it comes to navigating anxiety in places where they might not expect to feel anxious. I also wanted to give them a voice to speak their truths when it comes to relationships.

I have many friends whose parents never discussed relationships and sex with them. These are very sensitive subjects, and every person has their own belief system around them. However, I wanted to share enough that teen girls can make an educated decision should the only exposure about sex be from school or friends. Anxiety adds a new layer to relationships, and I believe if I had excluded them from this book, I would have done a disservice to teenagers who have not had the experience of having this conversation in a safe parental environment.

The key to maintaining your relationship with your child(ren) will be to have open communication. It's easy to want to be friends with your child(ren), and it's great to be friends with them, but first and foremost, comes parenting.

When you approach parenting with the thought that being friends with your child(ren) is a luxury and that your goal is to be a parent first, friend second, you'll be able to have a clear line in the sand. Children need us as parents more than they need us as friends, and it's important for us to encourage them to spend as much time with their peers as is healthy with their busy schedule.

For me, it has always been challenging to let things roll off my shoulders. My children are much better at this than I am. Thank goodness!

If someone hurts them, my mama bear instincts kick in, and it is "really" difficult for me to turn them off. I want to find everything wrong with that child and make sure my child recognizes it too. But that doesn't help matters. I've learned to instead evaluate the situation, be there to support my children, and help them make the next right decision to handle the situation or person with kindness.

One thing I've learned over the years, mostly from my experience being bullied in elementary and middle grades, is that when others are insecure and jealous, they find faults in others and try to make them feel less about themselves. Girls are notorious for this. Guys tend to either just move on or have a fight and be over it. But girls are unique creatures and can let things build and eventually someone is hurt. If a child has anxiety, they may already feel inadequate, and when someone says something mean or hurts them, they take it more personally. Girls may be less able to see it for what it is—the other girl being insecure and jealous. This is where parents come in, and where, as my daughter enters her teen years, I have to quiet my internal mama bear dialogue, simply advising and letting my daughter talk about her feelings and her perspective. I shared my advice from a place of kindness, guiding her to behave respectfully, not talk about other girls to her friends, and be kind despite how other girls may make her feel.

Trust also comes into play. It's important that your child(ren) can trust you to not tell the other parent what their daughter said/did (unless, of course, someone could be in danger). Also, explain to your child(ren) that they should proceed with caution and not trust the other girl right away if she does come back and want to be friends again.

Also, regarding relationships and your teen with anxiety, is the relationship her two parents have. This is a sensitive subject for me. I mentioned in an earlier chapter that my mom was only seventeen when she had me. My father was six years older than my mother. They were madly in love, but both had come from somewhat to extremely dysfunctional homes. As a result of their young age and family history, they didn't always communicate effectively, and fights ensued. I think my mom was insecure and lacked trust from her childhood experiences with her own parents, and my father had anxiety that quickly built to anger.

The dysfunction I mention in my parent's childhoods was significant. On my father's side, my grandfather grew up in an orphanage. His mother left him and his siblings. My great-grandfather had to work and could not care for them. The youngest, my uncle Donny, was taken in by an aunt. But my grandfather and great aunt Arlene were put in an orphanage. I adored my grandfather, but he also had a temper and was impatient. He also lost his arm in an accident. He was a lineman for Tri-County Electric and got into hot wires. Because he had diabetes, his arm wouldn't heal, and so doctors had to amputate it. It was his right hand that he lost, and, of course, he was right-handed. When I talk about having resilience, he is the definition. He learned to do everything with his left hand (including tying his shoes!). I was always amazed by this, and as a child taught myself how to do the same.

He and my grandmother were a striking couple and, I believe, deeply in love. They had three children very quickly and very close together. On top of the stress of raising a family was the fact that my grandfather had one arm and diabetes, which both came with challenges.

That didn't stop either of them, but my grandfather wasn't always the nicest to my grandmother. I still felt that being with them was a haven, and I loved how they doted on me, their first granddaughter. I was my grandfather's favorite, and he took zero initiative to hide that. I adored him. My grandmother was anxious (but wasn't diagnosed until my grandfather passed away when I was twenty-five), and she and my mother didn't always get along. This was a source of anxiety for me because I loved them both dearly. But as you know, in-law drama is almost unavoidable. I have been fortunate that I have always had a great relationship with my in-laws. I love them, and they took me in and treat me like one of their own.

My father adored his parents, but because my uncle was a sick child and my aunt was premature and the only daughter, (and my father was the middle child, strong and very independent), my grandmother's focus was primarily on the other two. My daddy told me one time that he never felt as loved as the other two. My grandmother told me that my father was her rock. There was obviously a disconnect in their communication with one another. I know my grandmother told my daddy that she loved him, but sometimes actions speak louder than words, and time spent together is also a factor. My grandfather and father were very close, but like I said, my grandfather had a temper and because of the way he was raised, he wasn't a big communicator when it came to emotions. You can see how both nature and nurture came into play for my father's anxiety.

My mother's childhood is a novel of itself. Her father left her mother when she caught him sleeping with her sister. When I say extreme dysfunction, this is it. Before my grandfather passed away in his eighties, he had seven wives. His love for women took precedent over his children. My mother tells stories of sitting on the front porch waiting for him to pick her and her sister up, and he never arrived. She spent many days disappointed from his betrayals. Her story is one of riches to rags. My grandmother worked, but as a single mom with limited income and nothing coming from my grandfather, life was extremely stressful. To top it off, I believe without a doubt in my mind that my grandmother had severe anxiety and depression, or was bipolar, but never diagnosed or treated. She verbally abused my mother and aunt.

When my sisters and I were growing up, my grandmother would go months to years without speaking to my parents. This upset my mother, and she tried very hard to have a relationship with her mother, but she never knew when her mother was going to be present or would disappear because she didn't like my father, or my mother had done something wrong. My grandmother still wanted to see my sisters and me, so we would ride around in her car, go get ice cream, or stay with her overnight. I loved her, but she also terrified me. She never hurt my sisters and me, but I never wanted to make her angry. We were to be perfect in behavior and appearance. She was the cause of many arguments between my parents. Because of my mother's parents' desertion and abuse, she struggled to trust, worried constantly, was insecure, and was very sensitive, often taking things the wrong way.

I can't imagine being raised the way she was or experiencing the things she experienced. When I was young, I didn't know all these things, but once I learned them, I was able to understand so much of her relationships with others and her need for everything to be perfect.

My father neither hit my mother nor abused her emotionally, but when they fought, the yelling was loud and frightening. I remember my twin sisters and me sitting together upstairs, all smooshed together in the middle of the night and trying to decide who we would live with if our parents got divorced.

I am not faulting either of my parents for my anxiety. I was born with it, but the fighting and yelling, the constant worry, certainly increased my anxiety. I tell you this not to put my parents down or share their dirt, but because I believe that our relationships as parents impact our children and their emotions. If they lack a sense of security, their anxiety will rise. If they sense turmoil in your relationship with your spouse, they will worry, and their brain will go to what ifs.

My husband and I don't fight very often. The only times we have fought, it was because we hadn't taken the time to communicate effectively, and frustration built up. One thing we've always tried to do was keep our disagreements and arguments to ourselves, behind closed doors. Yes, there have been times our kids saw us disagree or argue, but they've been few and far between. I encourage you to adopt this philosophy too, especially if you have an anxious teen and *especially* if their anxiety is a trigger of heated discussions between you as parents.

The bottom line is that your relationship with each other will influence the level of anxiety your child feels and the symptoms she experiences. I am not a relationship expert by any means, but I can speak from experience that anxiety levels rise when tension is in the air, and turmoil and chaos are in the midst.

Another aspect of the parent-child relationship is punishment. I do not believe in spanking. When my twin sisters and I were younger, my mom would spank us, and she would break blood vessels in her hand. As a result, she began using a wooden spoon, but the spoons would break. So, my father, who was an incredible woodworker, made a wooden paddle that was about 14 inches from handle to end and about one-and-a-half inches thick. The paddle hung from a nail on the kitchen wall and that became our source of punishment. To be hit with that was hell. The welts and bruises were painful, but that wasn't the worst of it. Emotionally, physical punishment is humiliating, and I believe it damages the spirit. I do not tell you this to shame my parents. As I said, my mom was young, and I'm sure didn't know the consequences of physical punishment. But, because of these experiences, I hated my parents at times, and I also lost trust in them. How could they say they loved me but then do that? My friends weren't punished with spankings, and in my mind, I was not a worse child than they were. Of course, I broke rules, came home late, talked back—normal kid stuff—but I believe conversation would have served a better purpose than spankings.

I will embarrassingly admit, and my son loves to tell the story, of the time my boys got spanked with a wooden spoon. I don't even remember what they did, but it was dangerous, like fighting in the street or something: I do not remember. I didn't spank them hard; it was a tap and they laughed, but the guilt that ensued was unpleasant. That was the first and only time I ever spanked them. I found that taking a privilege or a beloved toy away was enough for them to learn a lesson. Who knows, maybe my kids were just better than I was. Nonetheless, I hated physical punishment and never wanted to inflict that on my kids. I found that having conversations about the situation worked well, and they learned from that.

Your choice of punishment is none of my business, but I do want to emphasize that physical punishment is demoralizing, humiliating, and elevates anxiety. Inflicting pain on another human will not inspire or motivate them to behave differently. Once again, I bring communication into play. Communicating openly and having conversations that include explanations and listening will be much better for long-term relationships.

By the way, the phrase, *sticks and stones may break my bones, but words will never hurt me* is false. Words matter. And the words you choose to speak to your child(ren) will help make or break them emotionally.

One time, I was at my youngest sister's basketball game. If I remember correctly, I was standing and saying something to my mom. Mom looked up and told me that her friend told her I was stuck up. Those words stung. I was not stuck up, I was an introvert, I was shy, and I was also intuitive. This woman who called me stuck up was not a person I looked up to. I knew she was not healthy for my mom. My mom has co-dependent tendencies because of her childhood. It's like she thrives on worry, and she loves to be needed. This woman always needed my mom, and my mom spent a lot of time having to solve her problems. I was leery of this woman. I didn't trust her. If I wasn't forthcoming with her, it wasn't because I was stuck up. I was not super friendly because I wasn't comfortable around her. Those words, "you are stuck up" lived inside my mind for a very long time. This experience made me worry about how I was perceived, but it was challenging for me to be outgoing, especially around people I didn't trust.

If someone says something like that to you about your child, I think it is best to have a discussion with your child and ask them for their perspective on the situation. Ask before accusing or before assuming that what someone else said is in fact the reality.

It is important to remember that as humans we cannot judge another human by what we see. There is always more on the inside, just like you cannot judge a book by its cover. Making a harsh assessment or accusing someone of being a certain way can be damaging to the person's confidence.

Despite the sometimes turbulent and chaotic emotions of my childhood, life was good. There are fun memories, and my sisters and I were encouraged to be creative and run free with neighborhood kids and experience the joys of life. We were taught to work hard, love hard, and make the best of our circumstances. Most of all, we were taught to have faith.

Even though my father had a temper, he was one of my all-time favorite humans. He may have struggled internally, but he always made other people feel appreciated and laugh. People loved him and my mom, too. It was especially fun to watch Daddy tell stories and interact with others. Most of the time, the anxiety did not show in public. If he was in a bad mood, anxious, or angry, you knew by the hunch of his shoulders and the lack of spark in his eye. The things to take note of here are to watch for body language and realize that people can turn charm and emotions on and off. Being mindful of this may help you communicate with your child(ren), to read their mood or emotional state, and the reaction they may have to a conversation you want to start.

Laughter

Laughter://the physiological response to humor.

 The most wasted of all days is one without laughter.

E.E. CUMMINGS

IN RELATIONSHIPS AND LIFE, laughter is the best resource for joy. It may also be the best medicine for a healthy outlook and mindset. A life without laughter is like a river run dry in the Amazon Rain Forest. Life cannot survive without laughter. It does the mind, body, and soul so much good.

There are two concepts I want to focus on here:

1. Be willing to laugh at yourself.
2. Laughing with others.

Laugh at yourself. Instead of getting embarrassed and upset when you do something silly, or what you might deem as weird, stupid, or ridiculous, laugh. I've seen so many people, and yes, I'm guilty too, who take life so seriously that when they make a mistake, say something wrong, or do something embarrassing, they get angry, ashamed, withdraw, pass the blame, or treat someone else disrespectfully. The best solution is to admit what happened, and as long as it's not something that could hurt you or someone else, laugh it off.

Of course, there will be times when laughing it off isn't a viable option, like when you miss the game-winning goal or fail a test. I'm talking about those little nuances and mishaps that happen day to day, like wearing different-colored shoes to work, accidentally wearing a shirt inside out, wearing two different earrings, falling off a chair, running into to closed door, dribbling so fast down the court and tripping as the shot went off, or spilling a soda at the movie. These things just happen, and they happen to anyone at any time. We could get mad, cry, or storm out of a room, but what good will any of that do? None. Instead, laugh and let other people laugh with you. It will be good for everyone.

Even when those big negative things happen, don't beat yourself up. Life is too short to spend time beating yourself up over something you had no control over or something you can't change.

Please don't laugh at others or situations that someone might not find funny because they were amid the experience, and it left them hurt, physically, or emotionally. Give yourself the opportunity to share funny experiences, to watch funny movies or sitcoms, or to tell jokes. Bring laughter into your life daily. It will release stress and anxiety, and help you face every situation with a brighter outlook. With social media, you have access to humor, clean, safe humor. Follow people who are funny and brighten your day.

I love to laugh. It's my favorite thing ever, but I don't enjoy "dumb" comedy or when other people make fun of other people. You know what I mean—the kind of humor when people make other people look bad. That type of comedy makes me anxious because I am feeling sad for the person being made fun of. If you are empathetic and anxious, chances are you'll feel the same way I feel.

As with every other part of relationships, laughter needs to be initiated with kindness in mind.

Add laughter into your life and see what happens. Kind laughter makes you and others feel good. On those days when you are feeling especially stressed or anxious, scared, or tired, try to laugh. I can't guarantee it, but I bet you'll feel better even if you only laugh for a few minutes. If you can't find something to laugh about, make yourself laugh. Laughter is contagious. If you start to laugh, even a fake laugh, you will not be able to stop yourself from breaking out into full on laughter. Try it.

∼

PARENTS

Don't forget to laugh! One thing I believe has always made a difference in our family is taking time to bond as a family by playing games and laughing about memories.

Laughter takes the pressure off. If you haven't laughed together as a family, rent a funny movie, play a game, pull out old photo albums, or scroll through photos on your device. Have a food fight; get a puppy. Whatever it takes, just laugh together.

Some of my greatest memories as a child and parent are the times we were laughing together at the dinner table. Those are the times that bring joy, connection, and bonds that feel impossible to break. Even if that laughter came from launching peas off of spoons at each other!

Kindness

Kindness:// the quality of being friendly, generous, and considerate.

 Carry out a random act of kindness, with no expectation of reward, safe in the knowledge that one day someone might do the same for you.

DIANA, PRINCESS OF WALES

LET'S talk about kindness for a minute. Kindness isn't being nice. Being nice is picking something up when someone else dropped it. Kindness is from the heart, wanting to do what's right to make a difference in someone's life.

Kindness is accompanied by empathy. Empathy is when you feel what the other person is feeling. We've already talked about how hard relationship building can be. An example of empathy and kindness would be seeing another girl walking down the hall at school or down the street, and you know she doesn't have friends. She's not popular. You're afraid to invite her into your friend group because of what others might say. But you feel her loneliness and decide to talk to her, walk home with her from the bus stop, or invite her to your lunch table. You may catch slack for doing so, but you know that you don't ever want to feel that way, so you invite her in. That is kindness. Accepting differences is kindness. Thinking of someone else before yourself is kindness.

You never know when that person you are kind to might become the best friend you ever had. Always think of being kind as an opportunity that could change someone else's life, and yours. One little smile may change someone's outlook on life. You just might be the gift that saves them. Likewise, when you are kind, you might also find that you gained a friend, or now have joy in your heart that you didn't feel before.

People who are kind and empathetic make great leaders. It may take time to overcome your anxiety to be able to put yourself into visible leadership roles. Keep in mind that being a leader doesn't mean being popular. It could mean standing on a stage and speaking to large groups, being captain of the team, or having the leading role in the play. Being a leader means that you are kind and empathetic, and make people want to follow you. People want to mimic your behaviors because you are good and true to them, and you're inspiring others to be and do good, too.

PARENTS

Being kind is much deeper than being nice. It involves being considerate and truly thinking about the needs of someone else. If you exhibit this behavior, your child will learn from you and do the same.

Apologies

Apology:// a regretful acknowledgment of an offense or failure.

 You can apologize over and over, but if your actions don't change, the words become meaningless.

UNKNOWN

HUMANS HAVE difficulty accepting mistakes and apologizing for them. Asking forgiveness is even harder! I think this rings true to an even greater extent for people with anxiety. We are already anxious about the situation or scenario, and now we are supposed to somehow find the strength and words to apologize and ask for forgiveness. How? It's hard! So hard!

You cannot expect others to apologize to you or forgive you, if you aren't willing to apologize yourself or offer forgiveness. Here's the reality: We all make mistakes. We all say things we don't mean or are interpreted the wrong way. None of us are perfect, and we will need to apologize from time to time. Hand in hand, there will be a need to forgive. To forgive ourselves and to forgive others, whether they've initiated the hurt or reacted to a hurt we (accidentally) caused.

This is not to say you should apologize when being accused of doing something you didn't do. This is when good communication skills come in to play. Stand up for what you know is true. If you were misunderstood, communicate and emphasize your intentions.

Similarly, don't apologize when an apology isn't necessary. I've seen this happen a lot when unconfident people apologize for things, even though they had nothing to do with a situation. For instance, maybe you are running late (this happens to me all the time). Instead of apologizing for being late and providing excuses (there are always excuses for running late and many are unavoidable) simply say, "thank you for your patience," or "thank you for waiting for me." Instead of saying "I'm sorry," when you've made a mistake or there was a misunderstanding, you could admit you were wrong or say you misspoke. Or, when someone misunderstands you, you do not need to apologize. You can ask, "What are you confused about? I'm happy to clarify."

On the flip side, when you say something sarcastic or have done something repeatedly and your parents call you out on it. You say, "Sorry," but the sorry is not sincere.

You really aren't sorry, and don't intend to change your approach or behavior. You were frustrated or annoyed with your parents, and you meant what you said or did. Maybe a friend or one of your siblings has done this to you. Don't apologize if you don't mean it, and especially if you aren't going to change the behavior. Instead of apologizing, talk about why you said or did the thing you superficially apologized for. This will be beneficial for ensuring it doesn't happen again and that both parties understand what is happening in the relationship.

Another scenario is the "I'm sorry but…" If someone says "I'm sorry but" are they sorry or are they giving an excuse? Maybe it is a combination, but a true apology does not have a but that accompanies it.

When I was in elementary school and middle school, there was a girl who bullied the rest of us. On any given day, I could go to school, and no one would speak to me. This also happened to another girl; I wasn't alone. If you were on her good side, you were in; if not, you were out. And the manipulation worked in a way that if you were in, you didn't dare go against her. This went on for years.

When I was on the "out," I would write note after note apologizing.

I never knew what I was apologizing for, but I would apologize. I felt so sick to be isolated that I would apologize for whatever so that I could be back in the fold. But, when the other girl was excluded, I apologized by saying, "But, she told me I couldn't talk to you." No, no, no! That was not an apology, and it was wrong for me to not stand up for the other girl. What I should have done is apologize that I excluded her and ask for forgiveness.

The "buts" don't make the situation right, and they void the apology. If you are truly sorry for something, you accept the responsibility for doing something wrong. If you add a "but" after the apology, you are making an excuse or justifying a negative behavior.

Maybe you can relate to this. When I was in high school, there were a few times I did things that I did not have permission to do. I kind of went with the thought that it will be better to do it and ask for forgiveness if I get caught, rather than asking for permission and being told no. Inevitably I got caught. I would say, "I am sorry, but everyone else was going." That did not fly with my mom!

In this example, I was not sorry for going to the parties. No way! I wanted to fit in and did not want to miss out. But I was sorry I got caught.

Another example is a time when my friends and I all told our parents that we were sleeping at the other friend's home. Instead of staying anywhere, we stayed out all night. Let me preface this by saying I am a terrible liar, and I always got caught when I lied. The next morning, before we went home, my mom ran into my friend's mom at the store.

My mom said, "Were the girls good last night? Did they have fun?"

And my friend's mom said, "I thought they were at your house?" Oops!

This time when I apologized, I was indeed sorry for lying. I learned a lesson. I was also sorry I got caught. I was genuinely sorry for breaching the trust my mom had in me. (P.S. I hated being grounded too.)

Similarly, it is not good to apologize for something that you did not do. First, it is not necessary, and secondly, it is not healthy to accept blame and apologize for something you are not guilty of. When we take on blame or apologize unnecessarily, we devalue ourselves and begin to see ourselves as unworthy. Or worse, we begin to think we are bad.

Here is an example. Let's say you make plans to go to a movie with a friend. You get your tickets, popcorn, soda, and candy, and find your seats. Your friend spills her soda on her lap. You start apologizing because your anxious mind is saying *oh no, she's going to think this was my fault, so I better apologize.*

But it's not your fault and you don't need to apologize. Offer to help her by getting napkins, or suggest you leave so she can get a change of clothes and then come back to catch the movie. It is alright to say that you are sorry this happened, but if you didn't spill the soda on the friend, you have nothing to apologize for.

Remind yourself repeatedly that there is always a solution, but when things are not your fault and you have not deliberately done something wrong, assuming guilt and apologizing is not the answer.

The key message here: Don't take on responsibility and guilt that isn't yours. Your anxiety will be heightened. It is hard not to panic in these situations, but what will panic do for you? Absolutely nothing. Instead of panicking and placing blame on yourself, look at each situation as an opportunity to make a memory and laugh it off.

Admitting I am wrong is not something that came easy to me. I was stuck in the rut of perfectionism for so long that admitting I was wrong, and apologizing, weren't things I could do gracefully. If I admitted I was wrong or apologized, then I was admitting I wasn't perfect. It all goes back to being vulnerable. What I finally came to realize is that everyone is imperfect. We are all perfectly imperfect, and if we aren't making mistakes, we aren't breathing.

Now, I look at every mistake as a lesson learned. I don't fail; I fall forward.

So, if you are wrong or if you do make a mistake, embrace the opportunity to apologize and move forward from the experience with the new knowledge as stepping-stones for a better experience next time.

PARENTS

Apologies can be difficult, for everyone. Being vulnerable and admitting mistakes are often even more difficult for people with anxiety. If both you and your child(ren) have anxiety, this can add an extra layer of difficulty to any situation, but especially apologizing when you've had a confrontation, or hurt the other.

If your child(ren) doesn't apologize right away, give them time, but I encourage you to ultimately ask them to apologize if they have done something wrong. Being able to apologize and ask for forgiveness are life skills everyone needs. For people with anxiety, it is especially important to be guided on how to apologize from a meaningful heart space.

Likewise, if your child(ren) state that you hurt them, willingly apologize. I recognize that apologizing isn't easy. Pride and anxiety get in the way; we can make a million excuses. Like I suggest in an earlier chapter, do the next right thing and apologize. It will be an important step to ensure your relationship with your child(ren) continues to grow and that no hard feelings build between you.

If you or your child don't feel the need to apologize to each other, but the other thinks an apology is necessary, communicate. Have a discussion on why one thinks an apology is due. Sometimes, things are misinterpreted. Our minds perceive things differently, and misunderstandings are always a possibility. Instead of letting hurt feelings build, talk about each viewpoint, and develop an understanding of each other's perception. This exercise will help build trust with each other and security for your child(ren).

Trust

Trust:// firm belief in the reliability, truth, ability, or strength of someone or something.

> Trust takes years to build, seconds to break, and forever to repair.
>
> UNKNOWN

TRUST IS TRICKY! It is human nature to want to trust everyone. But, when we've been hurt or let down by others in the past, and anxiety is present, trust is hard to establish. It can be challenging to trust others, and even more so to trust ourselves.

The mind is such an amazing thing. It pockets memories so it can retrieve them when necessary. This can be awesome when we need to be protected from someone or a situation.

However, this can be a disadvantage because someone new that comes into your life may be completely trustworthy, but a previous memory or experience makes you skeptical. It's a *Catch 22*. Without trust, relationships cannot grow, whether with family, friends or romantic in nature. My best advice to you is to follow your gut.

If something feels off, your body is telling you to proceed with caution. The mind-body connection is miraculous and very powerful. If your memory is triggering something and you feel it in your gut, take it slow. You don't have to trust right away. If someone is trustworthy, you'll know it over the course of time. Reserve your inner most secrets for those you know you can trust.

However, don't share anything that could come back to haunt you. What do I mean by that? We all need someone to confide in. It's part of our human nature to need people and want to share, especially when we need advice. However, if you tell a secret to someone who has proven less than trustworthy before, they may use the secret against you later. I don't mention this to scare you or to cause you to hesitate to trust others. I say this to remind you to be cautious with what you share and who you share it with.

I don't believe people intentionally set out to hurt others by sharing secrets, but sometimes, it happens. I will share a secret with you now. Some people can be malicious. If someone becomes jealous, or you accidentally hurt their feelings, or someone else influences them, they may spill the beans on your secret.

The best practice is to avoid doing or saying anything that you will regret or could haunt you later.

Trust is one of the hardest emotions to secure in relationships. It starts with being honest with yourself and surrounding yourself with others who are honest, have demonstrated love for you, and appreciate keeping secrets sacred.

Judgment comes into play here, too. The people you can trust the most are the people who are not going to judge you, are not going to be jealous of you, and are not comparing themselves to you.

Any of these emotions will potentially result in the person sharing your secret. Quite often, when someone shares something that wasn't meant to be shared, relationships are lost, or at least damaged, and the trust takes years to rebuild. If you really think about the people around you, who can you trust?

Make a list of them and note why you believe you can trust them. and document any hesitation you feel as you write about them. If you have any hesitation, do not share your soul!

Who Do I Trust?	Why Do I Trust Them?	What Hesitation Do I Have About Trusting Them?
Mom	She has never let me down	Sometimes she doesn't understand me and gets angry when I can't do something because of my anxiety
Megan	She seems like a great friend	She's also friends with so and so and I am not comfortable around her, what if she tells so and so about me

On the flip side, be the one others can trust. If someone comes to you with a secret, and you know they are depending on you to keep it, do not share it. I know it can be tempting, especially if someone else is talking about the person, or asking you about the person or their secret. If someone has entrusted you with a secret, keep it. Spilling the beans on someone else's secret will leave you with additional anxiety. You become anxious over whether that person will be upset with you. You may wish you could go back in time to reverse the decision you made, which will make you anxious, too.

There is one caveat, however. If a friend is telling you something that could be harmful to them or someone else, you need to be very clear that you are going to tell an adult so they can get the help they need. Some secrets are not safe to keep. If someone you know is at risk, it will always be best to tell an adult, such as a school counselor, their parent, teacher, or therapist. If you have any questions at all, ask you parent or therapist for help in deciding what to do and who to tell. You can share the secret hypothetically to get advice.

It is not okay to go behind someone's back, but if someone is at risk of physical harm, help them get the help they need.

Trusting yourself is equally as important as trusting others. Anxious people tend to experience self-doubt. This is where knowing your values and morals come into play. The more you know yourself, the more you will be able to trust yourself to make good decisions. As I said before, trust your gut. Your intuition is a great source for weighing your options when making important and day-to-day decisions.

PARENTS

I've mentioned trust several times throughout this book. Every relationship needs trust to survive, and your relationship with your child(ren) is no different.

Anxious people have what if thoughts constantly rolling around in their minds, making it challenging to trust others. If your child(ren) confides in you, be sure you know their expectations with what you can do with the information, and what happens if you feel the need to have a conversation with someone else about the information.

If your child(ren) is in therapy, it is important that you respect the boundaries of patient-client privilege. Allow the conversations your child(ren) has with the therapist to be between her and the therapist. If they want to tell you what was discussed, listen. But don't ask her what was discussed. I have asked my children, "How did it go?" so that they knew I was available to listen if they needed me to, or if they needed to discuss or share something with me. Likewise, don't ask the therapist what was discussed. This is one reason it is best not to go to a therapist who is a friend.

You may be tempted to ask questions about their meeting with your child(ren). The therapist's session with your child(ren) is between your child and the therapist. If the therapist feels that your child(ren) is in danger or needs additional help, they are under ethical obligation to discuss this with you if your child(ren) is under 18 years of age. If not, then their relationship is strictly between them, unless your child(ren) has given the therapist authorization to share information with you.

It is difficult to trust this process. When you are concerned about your child(ren), you want to know everything there is to know for peace of mind. Therefore, selecting the "right" therapist is important, so that you can have a sense of trust.

I think it is also important for parents to emphasize with their children that they will trust them unless they give them a reason not to. Kids don't want to be watched 24/7. They also need independence, space to grow, and develop into their own beings. If you helicopter over your child(ren), they won't be able to explore the world from their own point of view or fulfill their own curiosity. Trust that if they make a mistake or fail at something, they will learn from it. Mindset work is important for you as a parent, too. If you constantly live in a state of fear of your child(ren) doing something wrong or something bad happening to them, you will increase the level of anxiety. Not to mention, the more time we spend thinking of something bad happening, the more likely it is that something bad will happen. Every human in the world needs a sense of safety and security to have peace. If you are constantly worrying, it will make your child's anxiety worse, and they will also lose trust in your belief in them as an individual.

Faith

Faith:// firm belief in something for which there is no proof; complete trust; belief and trust in and loyalty to God.

 We are twice armed if we fight with faith.

PLATO

THROUGHOUT HISTORY, faith has been important to individuals, communities, and societies. Some find it a source of comfort, some a source of conflict. I find it a source of hope.

Faith is one of those things that not everyone wants to talk about. Faith is a personal belief system that many hold close to their hearts, but don't share. Whether you are a Christian, Jewish, Muslim, Hindu, or any other religion, you have a basis of faith that you can turn to in times when you are experiencing anxiety. The key is to recognize the anxiety to know you need to pray about it. Once you have done so, faith can be a powerful tool to manage the symptoms of anxiety.

For me, as a Christian, I have always depended on prayer. I ask God for guidance, I ask Jesus to hold my hand when I am afraid, and I ask the Holy Spirit to fill my heart and mind with wisdom on how to handle a situation, or for guidance on how to overcome a negative emotion or experience.

A simple prayer I say each morning is, "Lord, please quiet my mind and calm my heart so that I may hear you and do your will. My heart and mind are open to you. Send the Holy Spirit to guide my steps, my thoughts, and words so that I serve you and those you desire me to help. In Jesus Name, Amen."

This prayer grounds me in peace. I know that if I trust God and approach my day in service, I will be able to find peace and calm, and have a full heart at the end of the day.

During times of high stress or high anxiety, I pray, "Holy Spirit, please come into my heart, and give me peace and focus so I can accomplish the tasks at hand and not feel so stressed."

Those who don't believe may hesitate or think those who rely on faith are a little strange, but faith is a mindset that can totally change your outlook and the outcome of your health or situation. We can find solitude in faith.

Prayer is powerful. God is ever present and all knowing. He gives us His grace, and will always stand beside us, in times of peace and in times of need.

When we look to God for guidance, He is always there for us. We can't see Him, but we can feel His presence, and the presence of His angels, and see the miracles He's created all around us. Sometimes, it is as easy as sitting in nature or going for a walk. Other times, it's reading the Bible. And, sometimes, it's listening to music or chatting with a friend.

> Now faith is being sure of what we hope for and certain of what we do not see.
>
> HEBREWS 11:1

Will you hear God speak answers to you? Probably not, but He will be speaking to you if you are mindful about what is happening around you and what others are saying to you. He gives signs if you are open to seeing them. Sometimes, they come in dreams. Other times, it's through the actions or words of others, or something you read. You never know, so be aware.

Let me give you an example. Once I had a big decision to make. I prayed about it constantly. I had friends and family members praying about it.

One day, when I was talking to a friend, out of the blue, she said to me, "I don't think taking that is a good fit for you." She went on to give me her reasons why she believed I would be better off saying no to the opportunity instead of accepting it.

Boom! Just like that I had the answer to my prayers. I call experiences like this God Winks. Here's another story that will help you understand how I know He's real and answers prayers.

When my daddy was sick with cancer, I was speaking to him on the phone while my husband was driving the car. I had a habit of taking my rings off and putting lotion on my hands. As I was talking, I took my rings off, placed them on my lap, put lotion on my hands, and continued the conversation with my daddy. We arrived at Target, and my husband pulled up in the front of the store to drop my son and me off. I got out of the van and went inside to do my shopping.

When we arrived home, I went up to my room to take my rings off and put them in my jewelry box. There were no rings. I had never put them back on after putting on lotion. I left them on my lap in the car, and when I got out at Target, they fell to the ground, in the rain, in the parking lot.

Frantically, I called Target to ask if they'd been turned into lost and found. No, they had not. My husband took an umbrella and flashlight and went back to Target to see if he could find them. No luck.

The next day, I reported them lost to the police station and put an ad in the paper offering a reward for anyone who turned them in. And I prayed.

My husband said we could buy new rings, but I didn't want that. I wanted my rings that had been blessed by the priest at our wedding. So, I prayed.

That afternoon, the police station called me to tell me they had my wedding band. I thought, wonderful, but I bet someone kept the engagement ring because it is worth more. For the next couple of days, I heard nothing. I continued to pray.

By Wednesday, when the paper went out, I was starting to feel like maybe it wasn't meant for me to have the other two rings back. But, on Thursday morning, I received a phone call from someone answering the ad. The man on the other end of the phone said his wife had found the engagement ring. He asked me to describe the ring to ensure it was mine. He told me his wife would be working at JCPenney the following day if I wanted to meet her there and pick it up. I got my engagement ring back!

We received another phone call about the anniversary band a week later, but we weren't home, and by the time we returned the call, the person said we had the wrong number.

That was okay. The insurance company replaced it, but the two most important rings were returned to me. And, I truly believe, it was because of prayer. God blessed me with the return of those rings because I had faith that He would.

Now, He is not going to give us everything we ask for. In fact, there will be some things He completely denies us because they are not in His will for us. And there will be other prayers He answers in ways that are not exactly what we asked for, but the outcome is far better than what we had expected or originally wanted.

This book is another example of a God Wink. For years I've had this book in my heart. I know there is a need for young girls and young women to know they are not alone (or weird, or crazy) in their journey of anxiety. However, I didn't know where to begin other than to write. The thought self-publishing was daunting and not something I wanted to invest time in. I knew I needed and wanted guidance on publishing.

It just so happens that I joined a virtual networking group during COVID-19. I am not one to put myself out there, but I decided this looked like a way to meet nice women and would be a good opportunity for my business. Well, I didn't get clients, but what I found was something so much greater: I met my editor and publisher. I scheduled a fifteen-minute coffee chat with her one day. To her surprise, I asked her about her business. She told me about her business, and I told her about my book. By the end of the conversation, we cried, and had a bond through our life experiences with anxiety. I knew I could trust her with my book and be vulnerable with her. Without her, this book may not have come to fruition, at least not in such a timely manner.

I believe God had His hands in this. He put me in the right place at the right time to meet Debby—someone who understood my emotions and purpose for the book and could help me get it in your hands.

Here is another story for you. This may seem a little out in left field, but it's something I've experienced numerous times.

Since my father passed away, when I felt down, or just needed him for advice or comfort, I've seen a red cardinal. When my grandmother passed away in 2020, the same thing happened. The day she passed away, I was visited by a cardinal. Then, in March 2021, when my godfather passed away, I said a prayer. I asked God to let me know that my godfather was in heaven and at peace, no longer suffering from cancer, and that he was with my daddy. The next morning, as I entered my driveway, there were two red cardinals in the pear tree. Two red cardinals. My father and my godfather. I do not believe this is a coincidence.

A couple of years ago, my son was driving to school. It was fall and we had had rain the night before. Bucks County is known for narrow, winding roads, and, on this morning, he slid on wet leaves going around a curve. His car spun out of control, hit a utility pole, and ended up on the opposite side of the road in trees. When I arrived at the scene of the accident, I couldn't believe my eyes. The car was obviously totaled. I couldn't believe my son and his friend were standing on the side of the road, unharmed. It was a miracle.

After making sure the car was loaded on to the tow truck, and my son and his friend were headed to school, I turned to drive home. At the end of the road was a field. At the edge of the field, a bald eagle sat looking at me. I got the chills. The eagle symbolizes courage, strength, and immortality. The eagle is also considered a messenger of the highest gods. I believe God sent the eagle to ensure me that He, and maybe my father, had been watching over my son.

The same thing happens to me through dreams. When I need advice or am struggling with something, I will have a dream in which the answer is revealed to me. I am not psychic by any stretch, but God has given me answers time and time again.

I could give you more and more examples, but I think it's best that you start praying and depending on God for your own answers so you can see for yourself.

He's there for you. If you ask, He will send the Holy Spirit to live in your heart to guide you and comfort you. God can glean joy out of despair, He can create peace out of adversity, and He can create beauty out of the ashes of smoldering losses.

God calls us to live in faith, not fear. There is never a time He is not with us to guide us. Sometimes, the devil sneaks in and uses fear to distract us from the security of God and keep us from trusting and finding peace. In times of fear, you have the option to turn to God's word. No fear can overpower God's love, grace, and protection.

 But Jesus looked at them and said, with men this is impossible, but all things are possible with God.

MATTHEW 19:26

Anxiety, fear, self-doubt, and insecurity can prevent us from reaching our full potential. These can squash our dreams and goals and prevent us from having true joy.

When we put our confidence in God, we can find strength to do things that will help us to reach our potential and find peace and joy. If we depend on ourselves or others, we will sit in a place of fear of failure.

In the table below, list your fears. Then, from the list of Bible verses, choose one you can recite when you feel each fear encroaching on your sense of security and courage.

Fear	Bible Verse to Give You Courage
Doing a presentation	"I can do all things through Him who gives me strength." Philippians 4:13.

BIBLE VERSES FOR COURAGE

So do not fear, for I am with you; do not be dismayed, for I am your

God. I will strengthen you and help you; I will uphold you with my righteous right hand. *Isaiah 41:10*

Peace I leave with you; my peace I give you. I do not give to you as the world gives. Do not let your hearts be troubled and do not be afraid. *John 14:27*

I can do all things through him who gives me strength. *Philippians 4:13*

Do not be anxious about anything, but in every situation, by prayer and petition, with thanksgiving, present your requests to God. And the peace of God, which transcends all understanding, will guard your hearts and your minds in Christ Jesus. *Philippians 4:6-7*

Be joyful in hope, patient in affliction, faithful in prayer. *Romans 12:2*

For the Spirit God gave us does not make us timid, but gives us power, love and self-discipline. *2 Timothy 1:7*

Whoever dwells in the shelter of the Most High will rest in the shadow of the Almighty. *Psalm 91:1*

In God I trust and am not afraid. What can man do to me? *Psalm 56:11*

What, then, shall we say in response to these things? If God is for us, who can be against us? *Romans 8:31*

For I am convinced that neither death nor life, neither angels nor demons, neither the present nor the future, nor any powers, neither height nor depth, nor anything else in all creation, will be able to separate us from the love of God that is in Christ Jesus our Lord. *Romans 8:39*

Be of good courage, and he shall strengthen your heart, all ye that hope in the Lord. *Psalm 31:24*

The Lord is my light and my salvation—whom shall I fear? The Lord is the stronghold of my life—of whom shall I be afraid? *Psalm 27:1*

The LORD is for me, so I will have no fear. What can mere people do to me? *Psalm 118:6*

Cast your cares on the Lord and he will sustain you; he will never let the righteous be shaken. *Psalm 55:22*

Finally, brothers and sisters, whatever is true, whatever is noble, whatever is right, whatever is pure, whatever is lovely, whatever is admirable —if anything is excellent or praiseworthy—think about such things. *Philippians 4:8*

You will keep in perfect peace those whose minds are steadfast, because they trust in you. *Isaiah 26:3*

Finally, brothers and sisters, rejoice! Strive for full restoration, encourage one another, be of one mind, live in peace. And the God of love and peace will be with you. *2 Corinthians 13:11*

Cast all your anxiety on him because he cares for you. *1 Peter 5:7*

Those who hope in the LORD will renew their strength. They will soar on wings like eagles; they will run and not grow weary they will walk and not be faint. *Isaiah 40:31*

NON-BIBLICAL MANTRAS FOR COURAGE

If you don't want to recite a Bible verse, here are some non-faith-based mantras.

- Action over anxiety.
- Fear can't hold me back.
- Anxiety doesn't control me.
- I've got this.

- I can do this.
- I can do hard things.
- I am loved.
- I am worthy.
- One step at a time.
- It is what it is.
- I can overcome.
- I can find joy.
- I can smile.
- I can laugh.
- I give others hope.
- I have hope.
- I am who I am and I'm okay with that.
- No one's perfect and that's okay.
- I'm perfectly imperfect.
- Just breath. Slow steady breaths.
- Stop. Focus. Breath.
- Stop. Focus. It's going to be okay.
- Stop. Focus. I'm going to be okay.
- One step at a time.
- I'll never give up.
- There's always hope.
- It's good to be me.
- I am beautiful.
- I am just enough.
- I am strong.
- I am capable.
- Smile. Just smile.
- No such thing is perfect.
- I'm not perfect and that's okay.
- Life goes on and I can too.
- If I don't believe in me, who will believe in me?
- I believe in me.

PARENTS

I believe that God called me to write this book to share His grace and hope with families living with anxiety. If, through writing this book, I save one girl from dying by suicide, I will have served my purpose. Yes, I am a Christian, but it doesn't matter to me if the person who finds hope instead of dying by suicide is Catholic, Protestant, Jewish, Muslim, Buddhist, or any other religion. I am simply sharing my faith because that is what has given me the most hope over the years.

I know I cannot do life alone. The comfort of hope through knowing God, knowing there is a higher power than what I am experiencing, has carried me through my life journey.

Faith brings me hope and peace. I can't imagine my life without faith. At my darkest times, I have relied on faith to find hope. Without hope, I couldn't find light. And light is what I needed to push through. I believe Christ died on the cross for me to save me from the depths of despair.

I didn't mention this in the teen book, but in my darkest days of anxiety, I had suicidal thoughts. During those times, my faith carried me through. If you've ever read the poem, "Footprints in the Sand," you can imagine the vision of Jesus carrying someone. He carried me through from darkness to light in those moments.

If you are a person of faith, practice it with your child(ren). Attending services, praying together as a family, reading devotions, and singing hymns can bring new life into your family, bring hope where there is despair, and light the path for your journey of healing from anxiety.

It can feel like God is not answering your prayer. I have experience that he is. We don't always receive the answers we want, or experience the outcome we desire, but God does answer prayer.

Because I have anxiety and tend to worry, I rely on prayer and put my trust in God to release the worry. For example, my boys drove themselves to school once they had their driver's licenses. Their drive was approximately forty minutes. I would have made myself sick worrying about their safety every day, so I prayed for their safety and put them in God's hands, and I went about my days. They were always kept safe. I told the story before about my son's accident in which he totaled the car. It was a miracle that he walked away from that accident with barely a scratch on him. The same for his friend. I have no doubt that my prayers were answered.

I share these stories because I know how hard it is to trust especially when going through challenging situations, especially with your child(ren).

Values:// who you are at the core, the core things that matter to you.

 Integrity is doing the right thing. Even when no one is watching.

C. S. LEWIS

THROUGHOUT THE BOOK, I've mentioned staying true to your values. Your values are who you are at your core and they indicate what things are important to you, kind of like your non-negotiables. Your values will help guide your decisions and how you live your life. As you make decisions, act on life events, and even navigate your anxiety, you want to demonstrate values and characteristics that are important to you so others can see you as who you truly are.

If you haven't thought about your values yet and are curious about what values are, you can find several lists of values online (refer to the References section of this book for a couple of options). To determine your values and discover who you are at the core, make a list of ten to fifteen values from the list provided. Then, evaluate your list and see where there is overlap. Narrow your list down to seven to ten core values. Again, look to see where there is overlap and evaluate which mean the most for you. Think about which value words resonate with you and move you. Then, narrow the list down to three to five values. Employ these values in the decisions you make as you build relationships and other social decisions.

Top 10-15	Top 7-10	Top 3-5	Why?
Faith	Kindness	Faith	Because I know Jesus helps me every day
Hope	Creativity	Kindness	I want others to know I care about them and want to make them feel valued
Gratitude	Beauty	Creativity	I love to create, it gives me peace, and joy, and opportunity to change the world
Service	Friendships	Leadership	I want to lead by example and help others find their way to a great life
Compassion	Influence	Friendships	I want to be a true friend that others can depend on and trust
Curiosity	Leadership		

APPLYING VALUES FOR SOCIAL MEDIA

Your social media interactions should reflect your values. Before you post, think about whether the content you are about to share aligns with your values. If it doesn't, don't post it. Likewise, if what you are thinking about posting could be interpreted wrong, hurt someone else, or be perceived poorly by someone, don't post it. Once you post to social media, even if the platform says it's only going to be there for twenty-four hours, it's there for good. There are ways to find everything, and you don't want something to come back to haunt you.

- Think before you post.
- Think before your comment.
- Think before you share.
- Think before you like.

Do not support posts that you do not understand or do not agree with, especially if the posts have any potential to hurt someone else. I do not envy you. I did not have social media growing up, and I am so grateful. I cannot imagine the burden of having to check it, having to comment and like what your friends post, having to worry about who will see it, or who will be offended. It is overwhelming and frightening. That may sound dramatic. It is best to proceed with caution before posting anything online or doing something that could be recorded and put out into the world. You could easily be misunderstood or hurt someone unintentionally.

The keys to not letting social media increase your anxiety:

1. Never use it to post your feelings about someone else.
2. Never post anything negative about another human.
3. Never post anything that a future boss could hold against you.
4. Never compare yourself to others on social media. Their lives aren't perfect either; they are only posting the best pieces of it.
5. Always post based on your core values.
6. Always think before you post, comment, like, or share.
7. Always remember that once you post, it's somewhere forever.
8. Always check in with yourself and practice the 5 Cs journaling method if you feel like you are comparing yourself to someone else.
9. Always remember that the grass isn't greener on the other side of that filter.
10. Remember, if you would not say something to your teacher, do not post it on social media.

In my opinion, integrity is one of the most important values one can live by. That doesn't mean everyone has to list it as one of their core values, but I do believe integrity is something we should all strive for. Sometimes it feels as though our world has forgotten integrity. We make exceptions and excuses for things that simply are not right: cheating, fraud, bullying, speaking half-truths, exaggerations, spreading false gossip, prejudice, sexual immorality, gambling, pornography, and so on.

We live in a world that is rigged to distract us and influence us in negative ways, to lead us astray and full of doubt. Submitting to any of the behaviors listed above will result in more and more anxiety. For example, if you tell one lie, you will most likely need to tell another lie, and then another, and then another, to keep someone from discovering the truth. When this happens, the stress and guilt of lying compounds, and your anxiety levels will increase exponentially with the thoughts of what if someone finds out the truth.

Lying is not worth the additional anxiety it will cause to keep a false story straight going forward. Life will be much better in the long run if the truth is faced upfront, no matter the mistake or how badly you think the situation may be. You may get in trouble, or you may hurt someone's feelings, but in the end, telling the truth is always the best decision you can make for yourself and for those you love.

It's time to stand firm and adhere to a high standard of values with no compromises to your code of integrity and ethics. If you need a basic reference for behaviors that are good, right, and just, refer to the Ten Commandments as a guide. If we hold true to these teachings, we can have a solid foundation for living with integrity and making good decisions that will positively impact our lives and the world.

It's one thing to be tolerant and accepting of others, no matter the differences between us. But it's something completely different to tolerate immorality, dishonesty, and injustices. As you are presented with decisions, make them according to your values and morals. Do not let the world determine what is right and wrong for you, because if you do, you will inevitably be misled.

Commit to a life of integrity and you commit to a life of excellence. It's making the right choice every time, even when you do not want to. Life is about choices, and the choices produce outcomes. If we want to live a life with positive outcomes and success, making decisions with integrity is not only important, but necessary.

 Do the next right thing!

Yes, we all make wrong decisions from time to time, but if we base our decisions on integrity, by looking within at our values and morals, we will be more likely to make the right decisions. And, when we do not, we'll be able to learn from them and grow as individuals. As we learn and grow, we'll be able to build better relationships and serve others as well.

PARENTS

Values are individual. Your child may have the same values as you, and they may have a completely different set of values than you. Either way, encourage your children to recognize their values and live according to them.

In the society we live in today, especially because of social media, people seem to forget their values and go with what they see everyone else doing on social media. People do what feels good, instead of what they truly feel and believe in their soul. If we don't live by our values, we lose our sense of self over time. Not to mention, if we aren't living by our values, what is keeping us grounded? How will we make decisions that are good for us in the long term?

If you aren't sure about what your values are, do the exercise with your child(ren). It is fun to do activities like this together and compare.

The same holds true with personality tests, the Enneagram Personality Test, and the 5 Love Languages® Quiz. When you compare your values and the other tests I mention, you can begin to see how your child is unique and where your differences are so you can improve how you communicate with one another.

Perfection

Perfect:// being entirely without fault.

 Strive for continuous improvement instead of perfection.

KIM COLLINS

WE ARE PERFECTLY IMPERFECT—EACH one of us. The longer we try to prove otherwise, the more unsatisfied with life we will be. One of my struggles with anxiety was associated with having to be perfect. I was terrified of making mistakes. It took me years to realize that mistakes are blessings because I have learned from each one of them.

If perfection was attainable, our world would be so boring. I've learned over the years that the journey with mistakes was more meaningful, and the mistakes introduced me to better opportunities than my original plan.

There are times when finished is better than perfect. My father always said that if I waited until everything was perfect, the "thing" I was waiting to do would never happen. He was so right!

It took me many years to accept that, but once I did, life got so much easier. Now, I can decide to follow a passion, dream, or goal and I do it. I plan for a while, do the research necessary to launch it, and then jump all in. There are days I feel like I'm sinking, but it is during those days that I find the most strength to persevere and get the task done to the best of my ability.

My best is never perfect, but when I use realistic standards to measure the success of the project or job I did, I can give myself a pat on the back and say, "at least you did it, finished is better than perfect."

To be able to accept imperfection and appreciate my best, I had to become vulnerable. I had to be willing to accept failure, mistakes, and not being the best at everything.

You don't have to hold the weight of perfection either. God has blessed you with unique gifts that only you have and only you can use to His glory.

The key is to use those gifts and not hide them because you fear you will make mistakes. Every mistake you make is a lesson learned. It took me forty years to learn that lesson, and I don't want it to take you that long.

Embrace your gifts. Use your gifts. And, if you make a mistake or even fail along the way, no big deal. Use the mistakes and failures as newfound wisdom for moving forward to serve others and achieve great things.

God uses us as we are, our imperfections, struggles, insecurities, and all. His plan is greater than our wildest dreams. Sometimes, the fear of not being perfect holds us back from simple things. I've experienced this many times.

When anxiety influences our thinking around perfectionism, it can prevent us from doing things, being who we want to be, building relationships, having fun, and enjoying life. The need for perfection to keep our anxiety at bay can result in a fear of judgement. If you notice, anxiety, fear, and perfectionism all link together.

The fear of judgment can result in saying no to invitations to hang out with friends, going to youth group meetings, joining clubs, going to parties, and more. The more you say no because you are afraid that someone will judge you because you aren't perfect, think you are weird, or not like you, you isolate yourself.

People get tired of asking and always being told no so they stop inviting you. Then, the cycle of negative thoughts comes in. *I don't have any friends, no one asks me to do anything, no one likes me.*

The reality is that they do like you. They wanted to be your friend in the first place, and they tried to be your friend. You now have a choice. Let the relationships fizzle out or start overcoming the negative thoughts. Ask people to hang out and invite people to do things with you, and gradually, you will be invited to things again.

There is an old saying, "Out of sight out of mind." If you are not willing to be present, to say "yes" to invitations, to put yourself out there socially, you may lose the opportunities to be invited to things.

Your thoughts will create opportunities or a lack thereof. Doing mindset work and journaling around perfectionism and the fear of judgement are keys to avoiding the loss of friendships or lack of invitations.

When you repeatedly say no to invitations, people will eventually assume that you don't want to be with them. That you don't like them. Realizing this is the farthest thing from the truth, you have the opportunity to demonstrate a mutual desire to have and maintain friendships.

If you follow your gut instinct with the type of people you want to be around and have on your friend list, you can trust that the people inviting you will not be expecting perfection, but the real you—the you that they found interesting in class, that they had fun with on the field, or liked when you met at a mutual friend's birthday party.

Remember when I said that it is best to treat yourself the way you treat others? You can also look at this as you get to treat yourself the way you want others to treat you. With that said, get out your journal and map out your thoughts around the invitation that is sitting on your desk. Decide, based on your thoughts and feelings, what you want to do, what you think is best for you, and what will make you feel happy, content, and most comfortable. You may ultimately decide you want to go, or you may decide it is best for you not to go. Take time to decide and don't rush your decision. You can use this model (CTFAR) to unpack possibilities related to your decision:

- Circumstance

- Thoughts
- Feelings
- Action
- Results

Circumstance	Invitation to a party	Invitation to a party
Thoughts	I can't go. They might think I'm weird. I don't have cool clothes to wear. I just got my hair cut and it looks terrible. No one will talk to me.	I can do this. I want to make new friends. Jane invited me so I know she likes me and wants me to be there. Natalie will be there, too. I can wear the dress I wore for Sam's party last year. I'll curl my hair.
Feelings	FOMO. Sad, lonely, miserable, uncomfortable, angry, and ashamed.	Nervous but excited, happy, and confident.
Action	Sitting at home by yourself.	Go to the party.
Results	Go to bed sad and lonely. Mom and Dad asking what's wrong all night. Not invited to the next party.	Have fun. Make a new friend. Received a compliment on your dress. Invited to another party.

If your thoughts create the outcomes in your life, which thought patterns do you want to adopt? Do you want to work on accepting yourself as imperfect just like everyone else, or do you want to continue telling yourself that no one likes you because you're not perfect?

PARENTS

You are not perfect. Your child is not perfect. You are all perfectly imperfect. That is wonderful because if everyone on this planet was perfect, the world would be filled with sameness, and that is not exciting. Work together with your child(ten) on accepting imperfection and embracing life as as you are, not on what is expected.

Comparison://the act or process of comparing.

 Comparison is the thief of joy.

THEODORE ROOSEVELT

ALONG WITH PERFECTIONISM COMES COMPARISON. It is so easy to compare yourself to others, especially if you spend any time in the online space. To navigate comparison, it is important to realize that no one is perfect, and the grass is not greener in someone else's life. It may appear that someone has more than you, is a better human than you, is prettier than you, or has more friends than you, but you do not know their entire story or what they have going on in their life that you cannot see.

If you sit in a life of comparison with others—what they are doing, what they have, how they look, their success, their journey, or any other attributes that vary from your own—you will be miserably unhappy. God made you to be you, not to be like any other human.

You have unique gifts that are only meant for you. You may view some of these gifts as a curse. I get it, you don't like every detail of your body: You want to be smarter, have longer hair or straighter hair, you want your anxiety to go away, or whatever other changes you are thinking of. God made you to be who you are and the way you are for a reason.

He has a plan for you, and every one of the unique traits He's blessed you with are the reason you are who you are, and these will enable you to live the life He has planned for you.

When we spend time comparing ourselves to others, we are not only wasting time, but we are wasting energy. In fact, we are attracting negative energy into our lives. Negative energy will weigh us down and prevent us from not only enjoying life but enjoying other people.

The next time you find yourself in the comparison game, do these five things:

1. Have compassion for yourself and remember you are wonderfully made the way God intended to you to be. Embrace your quirks and flaws as unique gifts. Journal about how each one of your gifts helps you be a good person and how your gifts have helped you help others.
2. Think about the blessings you have in your life and thank God for the unique skill set He has given you. Creating a gratitude journal is powerful. For each item in your life that you are grateful for, you will start to see more things to be grateful for.
3. Redirect your thoughts toward an action item you can take and accomplish today that will move your life forward. Maybe it is practicing for the sport you play, eating an extra fruit or vegetable, drinking more water, brushing your teeth an extra time, calling a friend, or giving someone a hug.
4. Ask yourself what you can learn from the person you are comparing yourself to. Use them as inspiration instead of comparison and a measure of self-worth. In other words, what are you comparing? How smart they are? How pretty they are? How athletic they are? They may have something you do not have, but I bet there is something you have that they do not. If you think they are better at sports, practice

more. If you think they are smarter, study harder or ask for a tutor. Comparison is only a limitation you are putting on yourself.
5. Pray for wisdom and grace. Wisdom to identify your strengths and gifts, and how to best use them; and grace to take messy action and accept mistakes and failures as lessons learned. Your action doesn't have to be beautiful and perfect. Master it later but take the first steps actively believing in your value. You have so many gifts to offer the world!

Comparison may also lead to competition. There is healthy competition, such as in sports or the best GPA. But, when competition becomes about who has the most friends, or who is most popular, or who has what brand of clothes, competition can become a problem. Competition can lead to jealousy. Once jealousy surfaces, friendships can be altered, or you can hinder your own progress.

Something I've learned over the years is that there is enough for everyone. If you are worried someone is going to have more than you, you are coming from a scarcity mindset. A scarcity mindset may prevent you from getting what you want. It is a negative mindset, and when there is negative energy, there won't be change or growth.

Here's an example. For years I've had a photography studio. Only recently did I invite another photographer to join me in my space. I was afraid that if I brought another photographer into my space, there would be competition. When I finally realized how silly this thought was, and how I could help someone else by giving them the opportunity to join me and decrease my expenses at the same time, I realized it was a win-win! There is no competition between us. We have unique clients, unique skills, and unique personalities.

You might be too young to associate this example with your life, but the concept of how being in a mindset of competition prevents expansion for oneself is universal. By bringing another photographer into my space, I helped make her dream of having a studio come true, and I was able to cut my expenses drastically. We do not compete; instead, we support each other, and we are growing professionally and personally.

The same can happen for you when you alleviate perfectionism, comparison, competition, and jealousy. Taking this action will help keep you in a safe and healthy mindset while decreasing your anxiety levels.

PARENTS

It is so easy to fall into a game of comparison. Have you ever been on the sidelines of a game, and you get stuck sitting next to the parent whose kid is the best on the team, the smartest in the grade, the most musical, and beautiful and nice on top of all of that? It's super hard to not compare your child to that child who seems perfect. Their child may be perfect, it's not likely, but the parent's bias sure is making it seem like the child is perfect.

Here's the thing: Your child(ren) may not be all the things that child is, but your child(ren) is unique, and how good she is at life now is not an indication of who or how she will be as she grows up. The key is to let her be who she is and by her side as she manages her anxiety in a chaotic world.

Your child(ren) is comparing herself enough. Every day she is faced with someone who outperformed her, is prettier than her, has more friends than her, and so on. If you start comparing her to her peers, the result will be more pressure on her, and her anxiety levels will elevate instead of plateau.

Grace

Grace: // unmerited mercy.

 Grace means that all of your mistakes now serve a purpose instead of serving shame.

UNKNOWN

GRACE IS a gift we were first given by God. He generously gave His son to save us from our sins and offer a home for us in heaven someday. It is up to us to accept God's grace. His grace is free. You have no obligation other than to accept it.

There are many costs associated with receiving earthly acceptance. We can often lose ourselves trying to be accepted in social circles, by teachers, peers, or even parents.

Grace is a gift we can also give ourselves. Through grace, we can accept and forgive ourselves, be less judgmental with ourselves, and live lives of joy.

Grace is a gift that, when accepted from God and from self, can change the way we approach our daily lives. Each day, start with gratitude and think of offering grace to yourself as a means of accepting yourself and all your flaws.

There is no perfect, and through grace, we can accept imperfection, believe in our worth, and live lives of service and joy.

Instead of getting angry or shaming yourself when something goes wrong, when you say something silly, or make a mistake, think of the fact that God still loves you, that it's okay because no one is perfect, and journal about what you learned from the experience.

God freely offers His love for you every second of every day no matter how you behave or think, and no matter what you say or do. That in and of itself should convince you that you can offer yourself grace to believe you are worthy of love, peace, and joy.

Self-compassion falls in line with grace. As humans we are going to make mistakes. There are going to be times we don't know all the answers. There will be things about us that we don't like or that are overwhelming (including our anxiety). It's during these times we need to offer ourselves compassion like we would offer to a friend or loved one.

When talking to yourself, be kind. Use compassion. If you catch yourself saying or thinking negative things about yourself, stop and rephrase the thought. Negative self-talk will not make you feel better or make the situation less challenging. Learn to forgive yourself and be compassionate. Tell yourself that even though there was a mistake made, there is a lesson learned and you'll move forward from here. It may seem impossible right now but try not to beat yourself up with negative self-talk. Creating models like the Circumstance, Thoughts, Feelings, Actions, and Results Model (CTFAR) and using my 5Cs journaling method can help you.

Learn the 5Cs journaling method I use to repurpose my thoughts. It's hard work, but once you implement the strategy, you'll see a major shift in being able to give yourself grace and living with self-compassion. As a reminder, here are the 5Cs:

- Catch
- Challenge
- Change

- Control
- Confidence

Read more about these and how to use them in the chapter entitled, "The 5Cs of Journaling Method." For now, I want you to remember that no matter how weak you are feeling, how afraid or anxious, it is okay to give yourself the grace to be present and learn as you move through these challenging experiences. Nothing heals or miraculously changes overnight. There is no magic wand; in fact, I think God's grace is the closest thing to a magic wand we will ever find.

If you don't give yourself grace and you beat yourself up over the emotions you feel because of anxiety, you'll never get better. Give yourself the grace to take it one moment at a time to discover ways to adapt your thinking and feeling to overcome anxiety.

In 2 Corinthians 12: 9, Jesus said, "My grace is sufficient for you, for my power is made perfect in weakness." No matter how weak or tired or overwhelmed you are feeling, Jesus is waiting to share His grace with you.

> Therefore, as God's chosen people, holy and dearly loved, clothe yourselves with compassion, kindness, humility, gentleness and patience.
>
> COLOSSIANS 3:12

PARENTS

We all need grace. It's wonderful to receive grace from God, but it's also a necessity to give yourself grace. You are going to make mistakes just like I have. It is counterproductive to beat yourself up over them.

There will be times that you lose your temper, or you say something you didn't mean. We've all done it, and we'll all do it again. We are perfectly imperfect so the mistakes will just keep coming.

And that's fine, because we will learn from each one. The key is to not sit in a place of guilt and shame. Forgive yourself. The sooner you forgive yourself and apologize, or make amends, the sooner you and your child(ren) will be able to move on.

When we do something wrong, lose our temper, say something we don't mean, or aren't present for our child(ren) when she needs us, we have an opportunity to apologize, or at least have a conversation with her about the situation and the reaction you had and why.

This isn't a time to make excuses. Own your mistake and discuss what triggered you and why you think you reacted the way you did. It is important not to pass blame as your anxious child is probably already beating herself up over the situation and thinking a million what ifs about what she did or said. By initiating and having a conversation about the situation, you will be a wonderful example for your child(ren) on how to move through life when the road gets rocky.

Curiosity

Curiosity:// the desire to know and learn about something, anything.

 I think at a child's birth, if a mother could ask a fairy godmother to endow it with the most useful gift, that gift would be curiosity.

ELEANOR ROOSEVELT

WHEN IS the last time you did something for the first time? Grab your parent or a friend and get curious! Find something creative and create a memory!

It's time to get curious and learn, then use what you learn to serve or help others. I believe that if more people got curious instead of letting fear rule over their decisions, the world would be a happier, more united and peaceful place.

People are different. God created us to be unique. Quite often, the differences are misunderstood. Many are quick to judge based on the differences, instead of trying to understand them. People are often isolated from social groups because they are different.

Curiosity allows us to see potential in differences. Instead of judging, avoiding or eliminating people because they are different, get curious. Develop a sense of curiosity that permits you to ask questions and invite them in. Their differences may be the ying to your yang.

Not everyone is a good fit for you or is meant to be in your life as more than an acquaintance, but curiosity lends to kindness, hope, and peace in the community.

Curiosity will also permit tolerance for differences. When we are anxious, we tend to fear the unknown. When people are different from us, we don't understand them, and tend to cast judgement designating them as different or not acceptable.

Instead of fearing differences, learn about the differences and try to understand how someone's differences add value to the world. Create a unique perspective versus one of judgment and exclusion.

It's often been noted that opposites attract. This is dependent on individuals but having differences can certainly complement one another.

PARENTS

Get curious together. Your child's anxiety is an opportunity to learn about anxiety and how you can navigate it together. The more curious you get about it, the more the two of you can learn together, and begin the journey of stabilizing and overcoming it.

Curiosity also comes into play when we look at the differences between our own children and the children of others. It's easy to fall into a habit of judgment, especially if a child is mean to your child or appears to have more than your child. Chances are that the child who is not being kind has something going on as well.

Curiosity has helped me in several ways. One, if a child is mean to my child, I get curious and ask questions: Did my child misunderstand, or was there a miscommunication? Is there an underlying pattern of behavior between that child and my child? Is the child who was mean to my child going through emotional turmoil herself?

We may not be able to get all the answers we are looking for but asking questions and helping your child(ren) get curious may deflect some of the judgement and anger that can result from altercations between teens. By asking questions and guiding our children in how they handle situations, we can help them become more curious and less judgmental over time.

Another way you can encourage your child(ren) to get curious is to learn about different cultures, races, and religions. Inevitably they will go to school or participate in activities with children who are quite different than them. Differences may trigger anxiety. If you notice a pattern of anxiety when your child is with children who are unlike her, or if she begins to avoid situations because she doesn't know the other kids, encourage her to ask questions and use curiosity to get to know more about them. A lack of knowledge leads to a lack of understanding, and combined, they lead to intimidation, fear, confusion, and possibly heightened anxiety.

> When is the last time you did something for the first time? Grab your child(ren) and go do something! You'll show them how to be brave, and you'll create a memory at the same time!

Hope

Hope:// a feeling of expectation and desire for a certain thing to happen, a sense or feeling of trust; to want something to happen.

 I am still far from being what I want to be, but with God's help I shall succeed.

VINCENT VAN GOGH

EVERY DAY IS A NEW DAY, a new experience, a new start. When you learn to be more compassionate and give yourself grace, you'll also start living with more hope. Speak of hope. What do I mean by that? Record your voice. We've talked about positive affirmations and mantras. Record yourself saying them and listen to them every day, at least in the morning and throughout the day if you need a reminder.

Just like writing is a powerful way to connect our minds, body, and spirit, so is voice recording. The more we hear our voices saying positive, calming mantras, the more we believe them, the more peace, joy and confidence we will experience.

PARENTS

As I mentioned previously, faith has been a source of hope and security for me. No matter where you find hope, I encourage you to lean into it. There may be moments you feel completely deflated from frustration and overwhelm because the signs and symptoms of your child's anxiety aren't abating. In fact, you may become exhausted. This is when hope comes in. Whether it's reciting a Bible verse, using a mantra like "this too shall pass" or "we'll get through this" or "this is temporary," come up with something that gives you hope to get out of bed each morning and face the day with your anxious teen. With the right help, there will always be hope for a brighter tomorrow.

Self-discipline, Intentions, and Creating Healthy Habits

Discipline:// control gained by enforcing obedience, or order, self-control.

 Motivation gets you going, but discipline keeps you growing.

JOHN C. MAXWELL

START with the non-negotiables of having a positive mindset and healthy lifestyle (see chapter entitled, "Relationships"). When your body is healthy, your mind is healthy. When your mind is healthy, your body is healthy. The two go hand in hand. It is important to care for both, not one or the other.

Let's start with thinking positive thoughts. It should be easy, but for someone with anxiety it isn't, and it takes work to develop healthy habits around self-talk. When you find yourself having negative thoughts or shaming yourself, make it a habit to change the thoughts. Build on a positive thought or mantra. For example, "It's okay, I'm okay. I've got this. It will all work out. I can do this. I am worthy. I am valuable." Or, say a prayer or recite a Bible verse. See a full list in the chapter entitled "Faith."

Two of my favorite verses to recite when I need to use self-discipline to catch and change my anxious, negative thoughts are Philippians 4:6-7 and Philippians 4:13.

 Do not be anxious about anything, but in every situation, by prayer and petition, with thanksgiving, present your requests to God. And the peace of God, which transcends all understanding, will guard your hearts and your minds in Christ Jesus.

PHILIPPIANS 4:6-7

I can do all this through him who gives me strength.

PHILIPPIANS 4:13

In the chapter entitled, "The 5Cs Journaling Method," I give you the journaling method that has helped me overcome negative thoughts and pushed me forward to a place of joy, contentment, gratitude, and confidence. It doesn't happen overnight, and it requires consistent, hard work, and commitment, but if you practice it daily, you will achieve it. I am not saying the anxiety completely dissipates or goes away. That hasn't happened for me, and if we are genetically anxious, it is something we will always have to confront. But it is possible to manage it and have more good days than bad.

Initiating self-discipline in your life will help you create and stick to routines and develop good, healthy habits. Some areas where self-discipline is especially important include eating healthy, exercising, studying and doing homework, being on time, going to therapy, journaling, and mindset work.

It is important that you set boundaries to accomplish what you need to do but also have some down time. Giving yourself downtime is a means of taking care of yourself, whether that is watching TV, hanging out with friends, reading, or taking a hot bath. The more you get into a self-discipline and self-care regimen now, the easier it will be as you get older and navigate harder classes, college applications, and job interviews.

Just remember that everything in moderation is best. You do not want to go overboard or become too regimented with your routine because you may become burnt out or even more anxious. The idea behind self-discipline and self-care is to help you navigate life and alleviate stress, not induce it.

PARENTS

Self-discipline is important for so many reasons, and I believe it's important for kids to learn this early on. It helps with study habits, placement on sports teams, friendships, and more. I want to point out that if your child is taking control, and trying to eat healthy and exercise, just watch for obsessive behaviors. It is not uncommon for children with anxiety to develop obsessive compulsive disorder. You want to be especially cautious related to an activity that when done excessively could result in harm, such as exercising or limiting food.

When my son started running to overcome his anxiety, it became an obsession. He couldn't run enough. By seventeen, he had done two marathons. Our entire family life was navigated around his running and him being able to get his long runs in. To save family chaos, we changed vacation plans and everything. I don't recommend this.

I always wanted to keep peace and have everything run smoothly, so instead of doing what we wanted, we sacrificed to keep him happy. Looking back, there are lessons learned. As parents, we gave into his anxieties instead of helping him navigate them better. It would have been one thing if a week of not running would have prevented him from achieving a goal, but that wasn't the case. This was him needing to run because of obsessive compulsive disorder caused by anxiety. I don't know if given the opportunity to go back in time that our decisions would have been different, but I think so. Knowing what I know now, I would have insisted on more therapy and had someone else help us figure out situations like that, instead of sacrificing the way we did. But then again, as parents, that's what we do. At least for us, we know how grateful our son was and what an incredible young man he is today, and for that, I am grateful. But, if I can help you navigate this better than we did, I'll be even happier.

Confidence

Confidence:// a feeling or consciousness of one's powers or of reliance on one's circumstances; faith or belief that one will act in a right, proper, or effective way.

 Beauty begins the moment you decide to be yourself.

COCO CHANEL

CONFIDENCE CAN MEAN different things to different people. Confidence is not meant to mean conceit.

You know those people who you see or hear speak, and you think, "Man, they are so full of themselves, so conceited?" We don't want to be them, but we do have a human desire and need to be confident.

Being confident comes naturally for some and not for others. I've often seen women move around their life with such ease and grace, and I have dreamt of living like that. Where did their confidence come from? Was it innate? Did their parents lather them with compliments and encouragement? How can they be so confident when I just want to hide in the back of a room?

The answer is we are all born with unique gifts, abilities, talents, and personalities. In addition, life experiences have the power to alter the traits that were innate.

Confidence is one of those traits that others have naturally accept, and use in their daily lives, while others lack it, or had experiences that limit our ability to be confident.

If you are struggling to be confident, the first place to seek it is God. When I became more grounded in my faith, confidence started to feel more natural.

God has given us gifts to use, and when we believe in Him and the gifts and the abilities He has given us, we are able to see how wonderful we really are, and how we can use these gifts to serve and live joyfully.

Likewise, you can journal around your unique qualities. You are you. Each characteristic about you is special to you. Journal around how your gifts and the things that make you unique and write notes to yourself about how truly awesome you are. I want you to become so confident that you can walk into a room without saying, "What if." If you find yourself thinking what if everyone is looking at me, answer with, "So, I look great!" If you find yourself thinking what if my outfit isn't perfect, answer with, "I feel great in it, so it's fine." If you find yourself thinking what if no one talks to me, answer with, "So, I can talk to people first and then they'll talk to me." You can control your thoughts.

When you have a test, study and prepare; this will help you with confidence as you take the test. Then, once you've done well on the test, use that as a marker for the next time the what ifs come into play. What if I don't do well on this test? Answer with "I did great last time and I studied even more for this test."

You can build your confidence daily. Use the same question and answer system every time the what ifs come into play. Look at past experiences and remind yourself of how well you did. If there have been bad experiences such as a bad grade or a loss of a game, quiet your voice around those experiences and focus on the good experiences.

Remember, if you accept that you are perfectly imperfect, you will be able to handle the what ifs much easier than if you focus on trying to be perfect, which is not achievable.

As your confidence grows, you will be more likely to build genuine relationships. Why? Because you will accept your authenticity, allow yourself to be vulnerable, and open yourself up for love and trust with others.

God created each of us for a purpose. He makes no mistakes. Every piece of your being is created and wonderfully made for His purpose. Take root and find hope in that. Believe in your value and have confidence based on God's miraculous creation of the one and only you!

PARENTS

Do you think we are born with confidence? I go back and forth. Are we born with confidence and experiences take it away from us, or are we not born with it and have to learn it, and we all learn it at different levels?

Either way, some people have a lot of confidence and others don't. But, one thing is for sure, anxiety influences confidence. When your brain is constantly saying "what if," it is hard to be confident in your decisions and confidence with yourself as a person.

You can help your child(ren) navigate confidence by reminding them to catch the what if thoughts and challenge them. The more your child(ren) catches the what if thoughts, the more she can change them, and then her confidence will rise.

Giving compliments also helps confidence rise; however, I do believe that when given too frequently, people will question the value and meaning of compliments. Remember, the what ifs are on replay. If you constantly tell your daughter she is beautiful, but she doesn't believe that or her anxiety is tripping her up, she may think *what if she's just saying that what if she doesn't really think I'm pretty*, or *what if she thinks I'm ugly*, or *what if she really thinks I'm fat*.

The key is to be aware of your child and what she needs in the moment. Whatever you do, don't give a compliment, and follow it up with a "you should". That will diminish any value the compliment had initially and make your daughter lose trust in you. Likewise, it's best not to give a compliment after a correction or suggestion that she might not want to hear. For example, don't tell her not to eat ice cream because it isn't healthy and then say those jeans look good on you. I know this may sound silly, but especially for someone with anxiety, back-to-back negative and positive feedback messages are confusing and influence trust in relationships.

The best advice I can give you to help your child with confidence is to listen to them. Give them your undivided attention; be present for them. That's it. The more they know you are there for them, and support and love them, the more confidence they will have in your relationship and with themselves.

Gratitude

Gratitude:// the state of being grateful; thankful.

 Acknowledging the good that you already have in your life is the foundation for all abundance.

ECKHART TOLLE

I SUSPECT that there are at least three things you can think of right now that you are grateful for. Am I right? Gratitude is a powerful tool for overcoming doubt, comparison, anxiety, and fear.

Start now. List at least three things you are grateful for at this moment in time.

Today I am Grateful For:	I am Grateful Because:
My mom	She always supports me.
My journal	I love having a safe place to share my thoughts and feelings.
My dog	Who doesn't need unconditional love?

Every day going forward, list three things you are grateful for. As you become more aware of the blessings in your life, you will see how stress and anxiety will begin to decrease.

You can practice gratitude in the morning as you begin your day before your feet even hit the floor, or you can do your gratitude practice before you fall asleep at night. Or do both. You'll be amazed at the little moments your mind will notice your many blessings throughout the day.

Sometimes those little moments are hidden. It could be that a situation could have been much worse than what occurred. Perhaps you received a grade you weren't completely satisfied with, but it could have been lower. You may lose someone you love, but maybe they didn't have to suffer before they passed away. Gratitude may not take the pain of loss away, but if you can find the blessings in every situation, you can have a more positive outlook on life and find more peace.

I want to encourage you to find gratitude for even the bad. Remember: Through the negative experiences, you will learn and become stronger and wiser. The more gratitude you have, the more joy you will find as you move through all types of experiences in life.

If you have food to eat, clothes to wear, and water to drink, you have three blessings. Maybe it's as simple as an opportunity to smile or someone smiling at you.

Having a heart of gratitude will ground you in the reality that no matter the circumstances, you will survive, and God will provide for you and bless you.

If you struggle to find three things to be grateful for, simply look around you. Look out the window. You can be grateful for something as simple as a blue sky or rain to water the flowers. There are blessings, both big and small in everything we do, have, see, and experience. Seek them and document them.

As you seek them and write them down, you'll start to feel less anxious because you will realize God provides for you, even when times are tough, and life seems hard. As we open ourselves to gifts, grace, and gratitude, we fear and doubt less.

If you want to take this a step farther, write your gratitude list in the morning, and at the end of each day, write three things that gave you joy. You will really start to see how positive life can be despite the obstacles, challenges, and anxiety that seem overwhelming.

∽

PARENTS

Life is full of challenges. There is no way to sugar coat it. What I've found to be true is that when I find something to be grateful for every single day, life is better. There will always be challenges, heartache, frustration, overwhelm, stress, and disappointments, but one thing is for certain, everything happens for a reason.

Even when things seem really bad, there is something good to be found. Maybe your child is having a really bad day on the same day you are having a really bad day. You might not want to deal with their issues at the same time you have to deal with your challenges. But, at the end of the day, you can be grateful that you were both together, safe, and you were able to help her, and she gave you a new perspective on the situation you were dealing with.

If your child totals your car, you can look at it as awful, get angry, sad, or whatever negative emotion, or you can look at it from a heart of gratitude, thank goodness she wasn't hurt! Thank goodness we don't have medical expenses. Thank goodness we have insurance. Thank goodness, I was able to go pick her up, or so and so lived close by and could get to her quickly.

Oh, there will be days when it takes longer to find something to be grateful for, especially when you work all day and have to then come home and deal with emotional stresses, help with homework, make dinner, sign consent forms, do the laundry, catch up on email, the list goes on. But, if you have food in the house, running water, or a bed to sleep on, you've got something to be grateful for.

The 5 Cs Journaling Method

Journal:// a record of experiences, ideas, or reflections kept regularly for private use.

YOU'VE READ the book up to this point, and now you are asking, "How can I break the bondage from anxiety, fear, and self-doubt?" The answer: There is power in writing your thoughts to connect your mind, body, and spirit.

Now, any time an anxious or fearful thought comes in and tries to hold you back, **catch** it and write it down. If you are at school, or not at home, document the negative thought in the note's app on your phone.

Once you have written down the thought, **challenge** it. What is the situation or circumstance? Is it a test? Is it a relationship? Is it an upcoming game or trip? Maybe it is as simple as what to wear or worrying about what someone else may think of you. The situation or circumstance is real and valid. No one can argue that. But your thoughts around it may not be rational.

After you have caught the anxious or fearful thought, work to **change** it. For years I've put off writing this book. Some of my thought work went like this:

Negative Thoughts	Rephrased Thoughts
No one will buy the book. I am not an expert at in anxiety. People will judge me if I publish this book.	If I write this book, people will buy it, this book will help others. There will be sales of this book if I write it.
What if people don't like this book?	People who have anxiety and need the book will love the book.
I am not an expert this book won't help anyone.	I have lived with anxiety my entire life and can help people if I share my experiences, thoughts, and feelings in this book.
I don't know how to publish a book.	Hire a publisher.
I'm not a good writer, there might be mistakes.	No one is perfect and it's the message that matters
What if I don't help anyone?	What if I help someone because she read the book and decided not to do drugs or die by suicide?

As you start to rephrase the negative thoughts, write the positive phrases and implement them as mantras. Say and write them every day. I am proof this practice works.

Next, take control of your thoughts by taking action. **Action** gives you **control** and will give you **confidence** to take more action to successfully accomplish your goals, dreams, and desires, including reducing your anxiety.

For example, I wanted to become an author. This book was weighing on my heart. I felt a calling to write it. I had to start by writing one paragraph every day. That led to one page a day, until I had almost 20,000 words and dedicated a week to finishing it.

As you walk yourself through the journaling activity, remember that having a heart of gratitude will permit you to open yourself up for more positive experiences and feelings in your everyday life. When we have a heart of gratitude, joy is present without you trying to find it.

If you struggle to find three things to be grateful for, simply look around you. There are blessings, both big and small, in everything you do, have, see, and experience. This book, journal, and pen are blessings. Blessings are everywhere.

As you seek blessings and write them down, you'll start to feel less anxious because you will realize God provides for you, even when times are tough, and life seems hard. Sometimes on the very worst day expressing gratitude can bring rays of sunshine to your life.

Here's a reminder of the 5Cs journaling method of breaking the chains of a negative mindset, anxiety, fear, doubt, and procrastination.

- Catch
- Challenge
- Change
- Control
- Confidence

PARENTS

Journaling has been a saving grace for me. I started with a gratitude journal, and now it is how I navigate decision-making, and my thoughts and feelings, which ultimately create my results. Writing this book is an example. I know God has been calling me to write this book for several years. For a long time, I used time as an excuse not to write. What was really holding me back were my anxieties and the what ifs around publishing a book about anxiety. What if people think I don't have any right to write this book? What if people think I'm crazy? What if no one buys my book? I had to journal around these thoughts so I could change them.

As I created a journaling model for the book, the one thought that pushed me forward is "what if I save one girl from dying by suicide." That thought has given me the confidence to quiet the other what ifs—and the confidence I needed to put pen to paper and get this book in the hands of families all over the world.

Think of a triangle. Thoughts are at the top, feelings at the bottom right-hand corner, and actions at the bottom left-hand corner. Think of arrows pointing to thoughts, which lead to feelings, which lead to actions.

But the arrows can also go the opposite direction: Actions that lead to feelings that lead to thoughts. I like the second as much as the first because if we are willing to take action, we can change the outcome.

Intentional Actions for Overcoming Anxiety

Important Note: Before making any decisions about the actions you will take to overcome anxiety, consult with your healthcare practitioner and your parents.

AS A PHARMACIST, I could write a scientific chapter on the medical treatment of anxiety and depression. But that isn't what this book is about. I do want you to know that there are treatment options, understand that there is no shame in seeking treatment, and accept the fact that to recover from either anxiety, depression, or both, you may require medical treatment.

THERAPY

Let's talk about therapy first. In my opinion, everyone at some point in their lives could benefit from therapy. Therapists, psychiatrists, psychologists, and counselors are all resources for the treatment of anxiety. They provide an unbiased perspective, they listen, and they ask questions to make you think of your experience in ways you might not have previously. Likewise, they are a haven where you can freely ask questions, state your feelings, and discover you are not alone in what is happening to you.

Cognitive Behavioral Therapy, or CBT, is what I've found worked best to manage my anxiety, but just like everything else, the treatment of anxiety is very specific to each individual and what worked for me may not work for you. CBT is based on the idea that what we think affects how we feel and behave; therefore, changing your thoughts can change the overall quality of your life. CBT is like the idea I mentioned earlier about catching the thoughts, challenging the thoughts, and then changing the thoughts. Using this method has helped me realize when my anxious or fearful thoughts aren't rational. It has helped me see when I'm being unreasonable and helped me to adapt my thinking to more productive, purposeful thoughts.

When I was in eighth grade, I was a member of the track team, and my event was high jumping. Back then, the bar that we had to jump over was a metal bar in the shape of a triangle. That meant it hurt like heck if I didn't jump high enough and landed on the matt with the bar under me, especially on my back. For those who aren't familiar with the high jump event, there are two stands on either side of a big mat filled with foam. The two stands have pegs that stick out so that a long bar can rest across the edge of the mat. The goal is to jump over the bar, not hurdle it. You literally lay with your back over the bar in the air and land on the mat. You keep going until you miss the jump twice. Then you are out.

I reached a pretty good height, one worth competing in events. But, after missing and hurting my back, my anxieties kicked in. The what ifs overruled the reality.

My mind was like a broken record: *Can't do it, can't do it, can't do it.* Not only did I not want to get hurt again, I was afraid of failing.

My daddy talked me through it. He had me visualize the positive experience of successfully jumping over the rod. I had to convince myself that I could jump over the bar because I had done it so many times before. Using the exercise before practice and before events helped me be able to compete again.

I had to catch those negative thoughts, challenge them with the reality that I could do it, that there was no proof I'd get hurt again, that there was no justification for thinking I would fail, and then change them to: *I can do this*. I can jump over that bar. I can count my steps to the point of jumping and stay in the rhythm I need to successfully get over the bar.

Still today, when I challenge my thoughts and realize my anxious thoughts don't make sense, I am able to change them and redirect my energy to a place of calm. Once I am calm, I can think again, and make sense of situations and move through them. But, if I stay in the place of anxiety, I am frozen, or can't focus, or can't do whatever it is I need to do, effectively.

MEDICATION

There are times when therapy isn't enough, and medication is necessary to overcome anxiety. There is no shame in taking medication for anxiety. It comes down to a choice. A choice to alleviate anxiety and have hope of living with less anxiety and be able to successfully build relationships, or, to continue to live in a miserable, fearful, anxious state. The need for medication, as well as therapy (or the combination of the two), may be short- or long-term. Individuals have unique needs and will respond differently. There is no one size fits all treatment option.

Sometimes, people with severe anxiety may need medication just to get their minds in a place where therapy can work. I know people who have gone to therapy, but without medication to help decrease anxiety, the therapist wasn't able to make any progress. This use of medication may be short-term until the patient is able to work with the therapist effectively.

If a patient needs medication, she will have to see a psychiatrist or primary care doctor for the prescription. Most of the time, it is a psychiatrist who prescribes anti-anxiety or anti-depression medications. Therapists, social workers, and counselors are not licensed to prescribe medication.

DEPRESSION

Quite often people with anxiety also have symptoms of depression. If you have a combination of anxiety and depression, there is an even greater chance you will need medication and therapy. Clinically, the combination of medication and therapy are likely to work better than either alone. Just as every human is unique, every person with anxiety has unique symptoms and unique treatment needs. Only a licensed therapist, psychologists, psychiatrist, or physician can make those decisions with you and your parents. Be open to treatment options, be willing to talk about your symptoms (in detail), and don't be ashamed about the symptoms or for seeking help. No one should have to live everyday with the overwhelming sensations of anxiety. Seeking help can help decrease the control anxiety has over you and enable you to experience the joys life has to offer. There are many treatment options available to help you.

CBD

Some people have found good results when using CBD oil to reduce anxiety. I do *not* mean marijuana. CBD oil is not the same as marijuana. Marijuana has psychoactive effects where CBD oil is calming, may help you sleep, and may reduce symptoms of anxiety. I am not making a medical claim here, but if you research CBD oil, you will find that people have had success with reducing anxiety when using it.

 Always ask your doctor, therapist, and parents before trying CBD oil or any other treatments.

If you do try CBD, use organic CBD products, and be sure that the manufacturer is transparent about the manufacturing process, where the hemp is grown, and what the concentration and purity levels of the product are. It is best to purchase CBD products manufactured in the U.S. to ensure quality and safety.

NOT SEEKING TREATMENT

You have options if you have anxiety. You can seek treatment, or you can continue to battle with or drown in anxiety. Doing the later may result in you trying to find alternate methods of trying to find peace and control. Such means include substance abuse, eating disorders, and/or isolating yourself. None of these will provide a solution and will add to the problem, and you may ultimately be in a downward spiral. If you have found yourself already considering or depending on any of these alternative coping mechanisms, please speak to someone immediately, such as your parents, guidance counselor, friend, or someone who can guide you to a therapist for the best options for managing the anxiety before it consumes you.

STOP FEARING JUDGMENT

The first step is to stop fearing judgment from others and seek help. No one worthy of your love is going to judge you. Your family, friends, and those who love you want you to be healthy and happy. If people judge you because you have anxiety, they don't understand it.

Anxiety and depression should not be considered any different than diabetes, heart disease, or cancer. It is a medical condition that just happens to affect the mind. It does not mean you are not "normal," or are crazy or a bad person. There is no such thing as normal anyway.

If anyone says to you, "Get over it," first recognize that they do not understand anxiety, and then, politely tell them that it is not that simple. Be firm, though. Ask your parents to take you to the doctor and explain all your thoughts and feelings in detail with the doctor. That way, the doctor can explain what is happening and encourage your family to get you the help you need. You get to be your own advocate. Do not let anyone push your feelings and symptoms under the rug of shame.

People who respond to you with "just get over it" most likely do not understand what you are experiencing and may not have experienced anxiety themselves. Despite the growing prevalence of anxiety, most people don't understand the signs and symptoms of it. They don't realize how debilitating and life-altering it can be. It may seem as though we are hearing more and more about anxiety, but the majority of people have not experienced it, and many who have did not realize what it was. Case in point, my father lived his entire life with anxiety. He didn't know what was causing him to react to situations so poorly. It wasn't until late in life that he finally sought help from a therapist and was put on medication, which changed his life. I think of all the years that could have been lived more relaxed and peaceful for him, and it makes me sad that he lost out.

Anxiety is in the mental health family, and people very often want to avoid any topics related to mental health. Again, be your own advocate. At a minimum, get your parents to take you to the doctor for the physical symptoms you are experiencing, so that you have someone that can help you get to the root cause.

Anxiety can cause physical symptoms, such as stomachaches, headaches, the heart racing, shortness of breath, and/or trouble sleeping. Sometimes behaviors can indicate anxiety is present. For example, people say they have obsessive compulsive disorder (OCD), but the difference between doing something for fun or for luck, like not washing your game jersey until you lose, is different than having to do something out of fear that if you don't do it, something bad will happen.

Any of these physical symptoms may require medical attention, but upon physical exam, your doctor may find nothing wrong with you. If that is the case, you might want to mention anxiety and/or ask for a referral to a therapist.

If you are struggling to get the help you need from your parents, you may need to ask a guidance counselor at school for help and intervention. You may also need to speak up and become your own advocate.

It is okay to fight for yourself, health, and happiness. It is also important to take a stand against the stereotypes, and advocate for yourself and others with anxiety. Your action may change the perception of an illness that has been silenced for too long.

Here are some other common things people who do not understand anxiety or depression may say:

- It will be okay.
- Just get over yourself.
- Why don't you go shopping, shopping cures everything?
- Maybe you need to get more sleep.

- Have you tried vitamins?
- Just take a break and everything will be better when you come back.
- Have you tried exercise?

Sure, some of these things may help a person with anxiety, but a person with anxiety can't "just" do anything. And how many teens have the resources to pick up and go shopping?

Grace will come into play when responding to such silly statements. It becomes a matter of forgiving people because they do not understand what you are going through. You can respond with, "I wish it was that easy," but I don't recommend arguing about it because if the person doesn't understand anxiety, you might not be able to convince them, and may risk offending them. Then, your anxiety and the what ifs may come into play.

HEALTHY HABITS

Diet and exercise are keys to overall health. If you are struggling with anxiety, limit the amount of junk you are eating, and focus on fueling your body with fruits, vegetables, and healthy sources of protein. It is also helpful to limit dyes, artificial flavors, and sweeteners. Artificial ingredients, processed foods, preservatives, and dyes may cause you to feel anxious or alter your behavior. Try to eat organic and/or healthy natural foods as often as possible.

Treat your body as sacred because it is. If you do eat candy, chips, or other junk food of any sort, make note of how you feel after. Are you feeling more anxious, irritable, hyper, or tired?

Write it down and keep track so you can learn the foods and products that you need to avoid in the future.

What I Ate	How I Felt
Ice Cream.	Happy but then sad and mad
A salad	Healthy, content, satisfied
M & M candies	Happy because I shared them with Mom

HEALTHY VERSUS UNHEALTHY FOOD CHOICES

HEALTHY

- All natural
- Organic when possible
- Fruits
- Vegetables
- Proteins like beans and nuts (if you are not allergic)
- Healthy fats like avocados and nuts (if you are not allergic)
- Lean meats and fish
- Whole grains
- Complex carbohydrates
- Water
- Green tea
- Vitamins and minerals

UNHEALTHY

- Candy
- Cakes
- Cookies
- Processed foods
- Chips
- Products with artificial flavors, preservatives, or dyes
- Soda
- Excess caffeine
- Sugary drinks or drinks with artificial sweeteners

EXERCISE

Do not discount exercise. When you exercise, your body releases endorphins, happy hormones. You don't have to run or do anything strenuous. A nature walk can bring a sense of peace and harmony to your mind and body. Get out and explore with a friend or family member. See the miracles all around, and you'll develop a sense of calm to reflect on when you are feeling anxious, stressed, or overwhelmed. Take a backpack with water and a book and sit amidst the beauty and the let nature's positive energy fill your soul with joy. Give yourself the gift of both exercise and relaxation.

If you are struggling to find an exercise routine for your body and abilities, ask your coach or parents, or visit a local gym who has a trainer for teens.

Most YMCA programs offer youth classes at a discounted rate. You can also find exercise classes and workouts on YouTube. Be cautious and only participate in exercise programs that you know are safe for you and your fitness level. There are many options for exercise:

- Running
- Walking
- Lifting weights
- Pilates
- Spinning class
- Yoga
- Barre class
- Kickboxing
- Self-defense class

The options are endless, and your choice should be based on your physical abilities, things you like to do, whether or not you play a sport, cost, location, and transportation options.

SLEEP

Sleep is an integral part to healing from any illness, and especially for keeping the mind calm. Many people with anxiety have trouble sleeping. The mind races, and it's hard to get to sleep. Even worse, it can be almost impossible to get out of bed some mornings.

Create a bedtime routine that will help calm your mind and body.

Journal, read, brush and floss your teeth, take a shower, use lavender-scented creams, say prayers, or recite mantras. Be consistent. The more you use a routine, the more likely it is to help. If you continue to have trouble sleeping, there are options for help, like melatonin or organic CBD oil. I do not recommend going straight to a medication, and do not ever use a medication without asking your parents, therapist, or doctor first.

Likewise, establish a morning routine. Set your alarm and get up out of bed right away. Do not hit snooze. I used to hit snooze several times, and I discovered that doing so made me more tired throughout the day. Start your day by journaling, doing a devotion, setting intentions, or saying affirmations. The more your body gets accustomed to getting up at the same time every day, the more you'll be able to get on a regular bedtime schedule as well.

Our minds and bodies love routine and consistency. The more you implement and stick to a routine and schedule, the more at ease your mind will be. I'm not stating that anxiety will go away completely, but these actions will help decrease it and help you feel better both mentally and physically. Exercise or physical activity may also help you sleep better.

One last thing (and it may sound silly): Name your anxious thoughts or that negative voice in your head. You know the one I am talking about. The one that tells you that you aren't good enough, you can't do XYZ, no one likes you, you are fat, you are ugly, or you are scared.

I call the negative voice in my head Janet, and I tell her to shush all the time. She's annoying, and if I let her, she keeps me up at night, brings me down, and prevents me from doing the things I want and need to do. But, I get to choose to silence her to move forward. Naming her made all the difference because now she has a persona and I'm not as afraid to stop her in her tracks.

Yeah, yeah. I know. It's easier said than done. It will take time, but just watch and see! If you give it a try, you will make progress. Notice, I said, progress, not perfection. Progress may not lead to the perfect scenario, but it is positive.

CREATIVITY

Creativity isn't a treatment for anxiety, but it is therapeutic and offers a release or escape from anxiety. For me, photography and writing poetry have been my go-to activities. At times when I've been very anxious, stressed or overwhelmed, I found relief by grabbing my camera and getting lost in the beauty of nature. I know people who use elaborate coloring books with designs, knit or crochet, paint or draw, cook, play an instrument, or make pottery as ways to clear their minds and ground themselves. When we get into a creative flow, our mind relaxes, and we can think more clearly, focus, and make better decisions.

You don't need to have money to invest in creative activities. Use nature, and a pencil and paper as your tools. You'll be using your mind, body, and soul to nurture and calm yourself, and you'll feel more grounded and confident.

And don't use the excuse "but I'm not creative." Everyone has the gift of curiosity, which lends to creativity. It may take time to find the creative hobby or outlet you love but start exploring the options today.

> There is **no** such thing as creative and non-creative people, only people who use their creativity and people who don't. Brené Brown

ENERGY PRACTICES

TAPPING

Emotional Freedom Technique (EFT), also known as tapping, is an alternative treatment for emotional and physical distress, including anxiety. The concept of tapping, also known as psychological acupressure, is that it balances your energy

EFT Tapping is similar to acupuncture because it focuses on meridian points, also known as energy hot spots. EFT originated in Chinese medicine and is combined with modern day psychology. Like acupuncture, it is based on the movement of energy through the body.

It is believed that energy flow keeps you healthy. When there is an imbalance, there is a risk of illness, or physical or emotional distress. Therefore, it makes sense that if the disruption in energy pathways is restored, there will be a shift in negative thought patterns.

The difference between acupuncture and tapping is that needles are used to release energy blocks in acupuncture where your fingertips are used to tap energy points with EFT tapping. Here is a list of tapping points:

- Eyebrow
- Side of the eye
- Under the eye
- Under the nose
- Chin
- Beginning of the collarbone
- Under the arm

It is important to note that tapping your body doesn't work alone. It takes recognition of the issue and acceptance of yourself as you are before and during tapping. For example, while tapping you need to recite something like "I am sad that I have anxiety, but even though I have anxiety, I accept and love myself."

Another difference between acupuncture and EFT tapping is that there are many more acupuncture points in the body. In addition, you need needles and a professional acupuncturist for acupuncture therapy. With a little bit of study, or guidance from an EFT tapping therapist, you can do tapping any place at any time.

To see an example of tapping, you can watch the TEDx Talk of Dr. Katie Nall, "A Technique to Eliminate Math Anxiety" (there's a link in the References section of this book). If you have any anxiety about test taking, you will find her talk especially enlightening.

REIKI

Reiki is another type of energy healing. Like EFT tapping and acupuncture, Reiki is used when energy is stagnant and not flowing properly through the body. Reiki practitioners believe that Reiki works by an energy transfer from the palms of the practitioner to the client.

Reiki is somewhat controversial as clinical research has not proven if it works. Like tapping, Reiki relies only on the practitioners' hands. Practitioners have reported that they feel an energy transfer, their palms feel warm or hot, and they will keep their hands on the client until the sense the energy is no longer flowing.

Just like every other treatment modality, the key is to discover if it works for you and is the right fit for your body and belief system, financial status, and time.

MEDITATION

I've mentioned mindset and how we can begin to catch, challenge, and change negative thoughts when they come in to play. Meditation is one way to not only pay attention to our thoughts, but to increase awareness of them and find an understanding of our thoughts and experiences.

If I am honest, to date, I have not been good at meditation, but it is something I am working on alongside music with energy frequencies to calm my mind and help me focus.

There is power in accepting silence and simply being in a moment of time. When we think differently, we can change our lives.

Remember, our thoughts influence our feelings, which influence our behaviors. There are nine popular types of meditation and include:

- Mindfulness meditation
- Spiritual meditation
- Focused meditation
- Movement meditation
- Mantra meditation
- Transcendental meditation
- Progressive relaxation
- Loving-kindness meditation
- Visualization meditation
- Guided meditation

Whether you choose meditation or other methods to help manage your anxiety, the key is taking action. Taking action is the only way to overcome and manage anxiety. You now have many options to explore to see which one is best for.

Conclusion

THERE IS an unbelievable amount of stuff you are challenged to remember every day. Things like brushing and flossing your teeth (did you know that flossing reduces stress?), doing your homework, going to practice, taking a shower, eating three meals a day, volunteering, practicing your instrument, working, and helping with chores. The list goes on and on.

Each item on the to-do list can cause a level of anxiety in and of itself if you let them. This book is not meant to be a cure all, but to give you some ideas and tools to manage the anxiety as it overcomes you, so you don't have to live in fear, shame, or anger.

Not one life here on earth is perfect, but you do have an opportunity to make the best of your life and live with a heart of joy. By reading this book, you've taken the first step toward creating a life with less anxiety and more happy, carefree moments.

I remember being your age and wishing time away. There were days I wanted time to fly by. It was all I could do to get through each minute as they dragged on. There were weeks I wished away completely. My message to you: Do not rush time.

It's hard to believe, but the older you get, the faster times go. Time is precious as we cannot get back what has passed. Once the moment is gone, it is gone.

Spend your time in the present, create memories, and cherish your loved ones, friends, and the experiences life is offering you. Tomorrow will worry for itself and bring what it brings. You have no control over what will happen in a day, week, month or even a year from now. What you can control is taking each day in stride, working to catch the anxious thoughts, challenging them, and changing them. With every change you make, the closer you are to becoming the you that you are dreaming and hoping to be.

Be patient, don't rush. No matter how overwhelming, demanding, and challenging life feels in the moment, there are positive experiences ahead, and they will arrive at just the right time for you.

Beautiful girl, you've got this! I'm cheering for you.

My prayer for you:

Dear Lord,
Bless this beautiful soul with a quiet mind and calm heart so that she may find your peace and understand the plan you have for her.

Life is challenging, but she now has tools to use to work through the challenges and hardships.

If she is struggling today or experiencing harm, fear, hurt, or any other negative emotion, please surround her with your angels, and protect her and carry her through to freedom and comfort.

Please guide her and give her everlasting strength and hope to grow into a beautiful, confident, kind, loving young woman grounded in faith and integrity.

In Jesus Name, Amen.

PARENTS

It is a lot. Raising kids, working, keeping up with a home and activities.

Having been on both sides of anxiety, living with it and parenting a child with it, I can relate to your thoughts and feelings. And I realize how overwhelming the day-to-day ins and outs can be. I want to remind you that there is hope. With action and faith, there is hope.

The best advice I can give you is to take life one day at a time. Focus on the here and now. Life moves at such a fast pace, and before you know it, your children have grown and flown. You may question whether it will ever happen, but it will despite the stress and overwhelm you might feel in this moment.

Don't let the past weigh you down. Give yourself grace when you have a parenting fail. We all have them. Let the future worry about itself.

You don't have control, but you now have tools and skills to navigate the road ahead. The keys are to be present, love, and nurture your child to the best of your ability.

And lastly, communicate. Talk to your child(ren). Be open with them. There is not a subject you can't speak to them openly about that they aren't already learning on social media. It is much better for them to learn from you than to assume what they see and hear on social media and secular music is right or good.

My prayer for you:

Dear Lord,

You have given this parent a child to raise and care for. You never promised that life or parenting would be all glory and joy, but you did promise that you will always love us and live in our hearts.

Please be with this parent today and grant them patience, and a sense of calm and peace in knowing you are with them and send the Holy Spirit to guide them in their words and actions to best help their child navigate the challenges of anxiety.

I pray Lord that my words have given comfort and support, and that each parent reading this book will have the ability to forgive mistakes and love themselves and their children unconditionally the way you first loved us.

In Jesus name, Amen.

Bible Verses Toolkit

YOU CAN USE these Bible verses to meditate on or to use for affirmations.

ANXIETY

Do not be anxious about anything, but in everything, by prayer and petition, with thanksgiving, present your requests to God. And the peace of God, which transcends all understanding, will guard your hearts and minds in Christ Jesus. *Philippians 4:6-7*

Humble yourselves, therefore, under God's mighty hand, that he may lift you up in due time. Cast all your anxiety on him because he cares for you. *1 Peter 5:6-7*

WORRY

Therefore, I tell you, do not worry about your life, what you will eat; or about your body, what you will wear. Life is more than food, and the body more than clothes. Consider the ravens: They do not sow or reap, they have no storeroom or barn; yet God feeds them. And how much more valuable you are than birds! Who of you by worrying can add a single hour to this life? Since you cannot do this very little thing, why do you worry about the rest? *Luke 12:22-26*

Therefore, do not worry about tomorrow, for tomorrow will worry about itself. Each day has enough trouble of its own. *Matthew 6:34*

ANGER, SHAME, AND FORGIVENESS

I knew that you are a gracious and compassionate God, slow to anger and abounding in love, a God who relents from sending calamity. *Jonah 4:2*

Everyone should be quick to listen, slow to speak and slow to become angry, for man's anger does not bring about the righteous life that God desires. *James 1:19-20*

I have told you these things, so that in me you may have peace. In this world you will have trouble. But take heart! I have overcome the world. *John 16:33*

But since we belong to the day, let us be self-controlled, putting on faith and love as a breastplate, and the hope of salvation as a helmet. *1 Thessalonians 5:8*

FAITH

Now faith is being sure of what we hope for and certain of what we do not see. *Hebrews 11:1*

FEAR

So do not fear, for I am with you; do not be dismayed, for I am your

God. I will strengthen you and help you; I will uphold you with my righteous right hand. *Isaiah 41:10*

Jesus says, "Surely, I am with you always, to the very end of the age." *Matthew 28:20*

COURAGE

Have I not commanded you? Be strong and courageous. Do not be afraid; do not be discouraged, for the Lord your God will be with you wherever you go. *Joshua 1:9*

Above all else, guard your heart, for everything you do flows from it. *Proverbs 4:23*

IMAGE

So God created mankind in his own image, in the image of God he created them; male and female he created them. *Genesis 1:27*

CONFIDENCE

In him and through faith in him we may approach God with freedom and confidence. *Ephesians 3:12*

RELATIONSHIPS

A perverse person stirs up conflict, and a gossip separates close friends. *Proverbs 16:28*

HOPE

He gives strength to the weary and increases the power of the weak. Even youths grow tired and weary, and young men stumble and fall; but those who *hope* in the Lord will review their strength. They will soar on wings like eagles; they will run and not grow weary; they will walk and not be faint. *Isaiah 40:29-31*

An anxious heart weighs a [wo]man down, but a kind word cheers him [her] up. *Proverbs 12:25*

Resources

These are just a few resources I found online. You can also ask a guidance counselor, pastor, pediatrician, friend, or use Google and search for therapist near you. It is important to note that some mental health practitioners take insurance, and some do not. You can contact your insurance provider to identify local organizations that accept insurance as a payment source. If the therapist you want to go to does not take insurance, your insurance company may reimburse you for partial payment. This is specific to each individual insurance policy and practitioner.

- **National Suicide Prevention Lifeline** 800-273-8255

- **National Suicide Prevention Lifeline** https://suicidepreventionlifeline.org

- **Better Help: Online Therapy** https://www.betterhelp.com

- **Talk Space: Online Therapy** https://www.talkspace.com

RESOURCES

- **Faithful Counseling: Online Christian Counseling**
  https://www.faithfulcounseling.com

- *Psychology Today*: **Find a local therapist, psychologist or psychiatrist** https://www.psychologytoday.com/us/therapists

- **Good Therapy: Find a local therapist** https://www.goodtherapy.org

- **I've Got You Project by Wendy Smith**
  https://ivegotyouproject.com/

- **Forever Frosty Foundation** https://www.foreverfrosty.org

References

"5 Common Foods That Can Trigger Anxiety Symptoms." 5 Common Foods That Can Trigger Anxiety Symptoms : Intrepid Mental Wellness, PLLC: Psychiatric Nurse Practitioners. https://www.intrepidmental-health.com/blog/5-common-foods-that-can-trigger-anxiety-symptoms.

"The 6 F's You Should Avoid to Combat Anxiety." Gut Psychology, February 12, 2018. https://gutpsychology.com/6-fs-avoid-combat-anxiety/.

"8 Food Additives Sabotaging Your Mood – Healthcentral." https://www.healthcentral.com/slideshow/8-food-additives-sabotaging-your-mood.

Anthony, Kiara. "What Is EFT Tapping? 5-Step Technique for Anxiety Relief." Healthline. Healthline Media, September 18, 2018. https://www.healthline.com/health/eft-tapping#technique.

Bertone, Holly J. "Which Type of Meditation Is Right for You?" Healthline. Healthline Media, November 5, 2021. https://www.healthline.com/health/mental-health/types-of-meditation#overview.

Brown, Brené. *Gifts of Imperfection: 10th Anniversary Edition*. S.l.: HAZELDEN, 2022.

Chansky, Tamar E. *Freeing Your Child from Anxiety: Practical Strategies to Overcome Fears, Worries, and Phobias and Be Prepared for Life--from Toddlers to Teens*. New York: Harmony, 2014.

Chansky, Tamar Ellsas. *Freeing Yourself from Anxiety*. Ashland, OR: Blackstone Audio, 2011.

"Core Values List." James Clear, June 12, 2018. https://jamesclear.com/core-values.

"Creativity as a Wellness Practice | Psychology Today." https://www.psychologytoday.com/us/blog/arts-and-health/201512/creativity-wellness-practice.

"Defining Your List of Values and Beliefs (with 102 Examples)." SoulSalt, January 26, 2022. https://soulsalt.com/list-of-values-and-beliefs/.

Experts, KidsHealth Behavioral Health, ed. "Fears and Phobias (for Teens) - Nemours Kidshealth." KidsHealth. The Nemours Foundation. https://kidshealth.org/en/teens/phobias.html.

"Facts & Statistics: Anxiety and Depression Association of America, ADAA." Facts & Statistics | Anxiety and Depression Association of America, ADAA. https://adaa.org/understanding-anxiety/facts-statistics.

"Fear | Psychology Today." https://www.psychologytoday.com/us/basics/fear.

"Fear." Paul Ekman Group, November 13, 2021. https://www.paulekman.com/universal-emotions/what-is-fear/.

Ferguson, Sian. "Is Anxiety Genetic? What Causes Anxiety and How to Feel Better." Healthline. Healthline Media, June 27, 2019. https://www.healthline.com/health/mental-health/is-anxiety-genetic.

"Food Dye and ADHD: Food Coloring, Sugar, and Diet." WebMD. WebMD. https://www.webmd.com/add-adhd/childhood-adhd/food-dye-adhd.

"The Gary Craig Official EFT™ Training Centers." What is EFT? - Theory, Science and Uses | PART I For Everyone: The EFT Tapping Basics | Official EFT Tutorial. https://www.emofree.com/eft-tutorial/tapping-basics/what-is-eft.html.

Gottschalk, Michael G, and Katharina Domschke. "Genetics of Generalized Anxiety Disorder and Related Traits." Dialogues in clinical neuroscience. Les Laboratoires Servier, June 2017. https://www.ncbi.nlm.nih.gov/pmc/articles/PMC5573560/.

Greer, Nicole. "The Best Way to Get the Results You Want: Think

Possibilities." Vibrant Coaching. Vibrant Coaching, May 16, 2018. https://www.vibrantcoaching.com/blog/think-possibilities.

Leech, Joe. "10 Top Benefits of Getting More Sleep." Healthline. Healthline Media, January 6, 2022. https://www.healthline.com/nutrition/10-reasons-why-good-sleep-is-important#The-bottom-line.

"The Negativity Bias: Why the Bad Stuff Sticks - Psycom.net." https://www.psycom.net/negativity-bias.

"Reiki: What Is It, and Are There Benefits?" Medical News Today. MediLexicon International. https://www.medicalnewstoday.com/articles/308772#what-happens.

Siegel, Daniel J. *Brainstorm. the Power and Purpose of the Teenage Brain*. New York: Jeremy P. Tarcher/Penguin, 2013.

Stahl, Ashley. "Here's How Creativity Actually Improves Your Health." Forbes. Forbes Magazine, December 10, 2021. https://www.forbes.com/sites/ashleystahl/2018/07/25/heres-how-creativity-actually-improves-your-health/?sh=109cb031136.

A Technique to Eliminate Math Anxiety. YouTube. TEDx, 2017. https://youtu.be/KZNdBxdNGIE.

Uma Naidoo, MD. "Nutritional Strategies to Ease Anxiety." Harvard Health, August 28, 2019. https://www.health.harvard.edu/blog/nutritional-strategies-to-ease-anxiety-201604139441.

"What Is Forgiveness?" *Greater Good Magazine*, n.d. https://greatergood.berkeley.edu/topic/forgiveness/definition.

"What Is Meditation?" Headspace. https://www.headspace.com/meditation-101/what-is-meditation.

"What Is the Negativity Bias and How Can It Be Overcome?" PositivePsychology.com, December 14, 2021. https://positivepsychology.com/3-steps-negativity-bias/.

Acknowledgments

I have so much for which to be grateful and so many people to thank for loving me, supporting me, guiding me, and holding me in prayer throughout the process of writing this book.

My husband John has been my source of strength for twenty-seven years. He has given me confidence and the ability to find myself and escape the insecurities and anxiety that held me back for so much of my life. If it weren't for him, I don't know where I'd be.

Joshua, your journey, above mine, inspired me to write this book. You are brilliant, resilient, empathetic, thoughtful, and kind. You inspire me every day to be better, to do better, and to love deeper. Your wit brings me laughter and your hugs bring me pure joy. I am proud to be your mama.

Samuel, you are my baby boy who brings joy to my life that I can't explain. Your journey has been one of struggle and triumph. You too have demonstrated great resilience. You are a kind, generous, empathetic soul, and I adore you and cherish the light you shine in my life. You are my sunshine, and I am proud to be your mother.

Grace, my baby girl, my only daughter. You are my blessing from heaven, a true gift from God. Your journey is only still beginning. You are my joy, my purpose, and my heart. You are everything I wanted to be in a teen girl, and I love to watch you move through life. You hold my heart, baby girl. I am proud to be your mommy.

Mom, I love you. In many ways we grew up together. Many times, in my life, you knew when I needed you. You've been an example of perseverance and always gave me the green light to follow my dreams. Thank you for sharing your creativity and encouraging me to embrace mine too. I want the best for you, and for you to find true joy and life without worry.

Daddy, you are reading this from heaven. How blessed am I to have had you for thirty-five years! I wish we'd known then what I know now. You taught me more than you can imagine about strength, resilience, humility, vulnerability, and love. Forehead kisses, until we meet again.

My sisters, Annette, Jeannette, and Lizzy. You are my rocks, my confidantes, my soulmates. I love you all more than you'll ever know. I am grateful for having you on this journey with me. You inspire me and give me strength every day.

My friends. I've been blessed to have so many strong women in life who have loved me despite my faults, insecurities, and anxiety. My college girls, Susan, Karen G, Carla, Karen D, and Angie. Our bond of sisterhood will last forever. I am grateful that through it all you still love me. Margaret and Suzanne, you had to move away, but our friendships and the similarities in our journeys have not only inspired me, but given me strength, encouragement, and wisdom beyond my wildest dreams. You are always just a phone call away, and for that I am grateful. Distance doesn't deter true friendship. Michele, my mermaid sister, you've given me the permission to be me and to stand for what's right and true and meaningful. Jen, you make me laugh and I love sharing the journey of motherhood with you. Missy, you are my sister in faith and living this life parallel with you has given me strength, love, and so much laughter. There are many more of you who mean the world to me, you know who you are. If I haven't mentioned you, it isn't because I don't love, adore, and appreciate you. But I am limited to space and time.

Bob and Robin, my Godfather and sister through friendship. You've taught me that it is what it is, and that family is family and everything that matters. I miss you every day, Godfather, but am ever grateful for the lessons you taught me, the faith your shared with me, and the love you showered on John, Josh, Sam, Grace, and me.

Deborah Kevin, I can't thank you enough for joining me on this journey. For carrying me through when I wanted to quit. Your guidance, teaching, and support are the reason this book came to fruition. God put you in my path for a reason. The day we connected for virtual coffee is a day that is permanently embedded in my mind and heart. It changed my life and hopefully the lives of many. Thank you for your gift of love, support, wisdom, and your belief in this project.

For my advanced readers and reviewers, a very special thank you. You gave me peace in my vulnerability. Your time was much appreciated and I am forever grateful for your love and support of this project.

Readers, without you this book has no purpose. Thank you for trusting me with your time. It is my dream that you will find hope from these pages and that you will have a better, safer, more joyful future because of what I've shared. I am truly grateful for each of you.

Lastly, Tamra Andress, a God Wink connected us and for that my faith and business journey were transformed. Thank you for sharing your soul with me and my readers.

About the Author

Dr. Robyn Graham is an anxious introvert on a mission to help teen girls go from feeling anxious to relentless by sharing her life-long journey with anxiety and the tools and resources that helped her not only survive but thrive. As a clinical pharmacist, professional photographer, brand strategist, and business coach, Robyn has witnessed both the clinical and social complications of anxiety and how it holds people, especially girls and women, back from achieving their goals and dreams. Robyn is a mom to Joshua, Samuel, and Grace, wife to Dr. John Graham, dog mom to Stella and Kona, and a daughter, sister, aunt, and friend. This is her first book.

facebook.com/therobyngraham
instagram.com/therobyngraham
twitter.com/therobyngraham
linkedin.com/in/therobyngraham

About the Publisher

Highlander Press, founded in 2019, is a mid-sized publishing company committed to sharing big ideas and changing the world through words.

Highlander Press guides authors through the publishing, launching, and promoting process and beyond, focusing on ensuring they have impactful books of which they are proud, making a long-time dream come true. Having authored a book improves confidence, creates clarity, and ensures that your story and expertise are available to those who need them.

What makes Highlander Press unique is its business model focuses on building strong, collaborative relationships with other women-owned businesses, which specialize in some aspect of the publishing industry, such as graphic design, book marketing, book launching, copyrights, and publicity. The mantra "a rising tide lifts all boats" is one they embrace. You can find their latest publications and submission guidelines at https://highlanderpressbooks.com.

facebook.com/highlanderpress
instagram.com/highlanderpress
linkedin.com/in/highlanderpress

www.ingramcontent.com/pod-product-compliance
Lightning Source LLC
Chambersburg PA
CBHW071413070526
44578CB00003B/566